HOW DO YOU SHARE THE GOSPEL IN OUR CULTURE?

Important Principles Every
Christian Should Know

Tim Alsup

Cross-Shaped Publishing

Cross-Shaped Publishing
Arlington, TN 38002

Scripture quotations taken from the (NASB®) New American Standard Bible®, Copyright © 1960, 1962, 1963, 1968, 1971, 1972, 1973, 1975, 1977, 1995 by The Lockman Foundation. Used by permission. All rights reserved. lockman.org

Cover Design by Melissa Ellis Smith, Memphis, TN

How Do You Share the Gospel in Our Culture? / Tim Alsup
ISBN: 978-8-218-68859-2 (Cross-Shaped Publishing)

CONTENTS

ACKNOWLEDGEMENTS

I am extremely thankful for *the Great Oaks Church of Christ eldership and church family*, for their support of my continuing education (which led to this evangelism study), and even more for their constant encouragement to my ministry and my family. I appreciate those at Great Oaks who participated in my doctoral dissertation project in various ways, as we explored post-Christian evangelism in classes and activities. I am thankful we were able to pursue this project together, and I am hopeful it planted seeds that continue to make us more effective in sharing the gospel. I pray that through this book it will do the same for many others.

Special thanks to those who read and edited this manuscript at different phases: *Debra Wright, Philip Slate, Chris Hill, and Matthew Mitchell*. Your corrections and feedback were invaluable, and you have helped make this book much better than it would have been otherwise.

Most of all, thank you to *my family*: to our children, Riley, Eian, and Reese, and especially to my wife, Arinne, for your constant love and support in ministry and everything else we have pursued in our life together.

¹⁸ And Jesus came up and spoke to them, saying, "All authority has been given to Me in heaven and on earth.

¹⁹ Go therefore and make disciples of all the nations, baptizing them in the name of the Father and the Son and the Holy Spirit,

²⁰ teaching them to observe all that I commanded you; and lo, I am with you always, even to the end of the age."

—Matthew 28:18-20

Introduction:
How Do You Share the Gospel
in Our Culture?

American Christians realized their culture was changing. After decades of church growth in the mid-1900s, routine efforts to share the gospel suddenly became less effective. People seemed disinterested, too busy, too skeptical, or too angry. By the time the early 2000s came around, the concern among Christians reached a steady boil. Most religious groups in America were declining in numbers. American media and higher education institutions appeared intent on discouraging religious faith, celebrating anyone who criticized the truthfulness or relevance of Christianity. Some churches suggested that we needed to change the Christian message—at least the parts our society disliked—to keep American Christianity from disappearing entirely, an alarmist attitude that seemed to betray a greater trust in culture than in God. The cultural ethos was going in the wrong direction. Eventually, one research project declared we had witnessed the largest and fastest religious shift in American history—a movement *away* from God, as millions of Americans drifted from professing Christianity into the "dechurched" category.[1]

Within this unprecedented cultural shift, many Christians got to work, exploring whether evangelism could still be successful in a culture increasingly described as "post-Christian" (meaning that Christianity was no longer the dominant cultural force it used to be). A wave of literature about evangelism rose up from a variety of denominational backgrounds:

books, research projects, articles, statistics, dissertations. Religious universities re-discovered the importance of studying evangelism on an academic level, after ignoring the topic for several generations.[2] Writers and scholars realized that engaging the culture had become a high-priority issue for Christians, who sought ways to share the gospel more effectively. What have those studies revealed?

The Question Behind This Book

When I began work on my doctoral dissertation, we were advised to choose a topic we were passionate about, given the countless hours we would spend reading and writing on the subject. I chose evangelism. After all, like many ministers, I was first drawn to ministry by a conviction that Christianity is true and a desire to share that truth with others. And whenever I reflect on how I can grow both in faith and ministry, evangelism is often at the forefront of my thoughts: I have felt the frustrations of our less-receptive culture like everyone else, so I regularly consider how I can better encourage others to follow God and how our church family can be more effective as well. Therefore, I chose evangelism as my dissertation topic, hoping to personally grow in this area and learn to better equip other Christians as well.

As I worked through the vast amount of contemporary evangelism literature, my focus narrowed and I began to ask the question hinted at above: among all the studies on evangelism and our culture in the past few decades, what have we found to be helpful? Seeking answers to that question, I wanted to read all I could from the mountain of evangelism writings, looking for consistent themes. I wanted to understand the challenges, and to know if there were reproducible best practices or important mindset shifts that helped in evangelism. And of course, I wanted to make sure that anything I accepted was faithful to what God has taught in Scripture.

Following that line of study, my narrowed-down dissertation topic became "effective evangelism in post-Christian culture." As I identified common themes from contemporary evangelism writings, I sought to distill them into a set of principles for sharing the gospel in our culture.[3] This book presents the results of that study, and I am happy to report that there is plenty of good news: people are finding that many non-Christians in our culture are open to Christianity, effective evangelism still takes place, and there are indeed some best practices and mindset shifts we can learn. I am also happy to share that these themes resonate with my experience in life and ministry. In other words, I am a believer that what you will find in this book is effective—I have seen these principles play out in real life. And still more good news: I am especially pleased to share that these themes are all rooted in Scripture.

Some of these principles are biblical attitudes we must "reclaim" in our daily habits. Some are simply understanding how people are different today than they were a couple of generations ago, requiring us to show wisdom and share the gospel with our changing culture in mind. Some are ways of thinking "bigger" about sharing the gospel, at least bigger than the stereotype of it-all-depends-on-me evangelism.

Equipping Christians to Share the Gospel

I have personally found this study to be both hopeful and helpful, and I pray you will also.

If you are interested in evangelism in our changing culture, this book is for you. Although the study originated as an academic enterprise, this book aims to be beneficial to all Christians. As I completed my dissertation, I felt I had learned things that I wished every Christian could know, and I imagined what could happen if we multiplied the number of Christians practicing these principles in their daily lives. I wanted to share the findings with other Christians as best I could. Although my dissertation drew from numerous sources, including a substantial amount of scholarly social science research, I wanted to consolidate the material and state the concepts in clear language that all Christians could understand. As I shared the reshaped versions of this material in different contexts—in Bible classes and sermons, in gatherings designed to equip church leaders, in evangelism seminars—people consistently gave positive feedback on the value of the study and the need to equip all Christians with these post-Christian evangelism principles. I decided to put the material into book form, believing it can equip Christians to engage our post-Christian culture more effectively.

I am convinced that most Christians care deeply about sharing the gospel in our culture. You notice the interest level rise whenever the topic comes up in Bible classes, sermons, or conversations. The gospel is the most important message in the world, changing our lives and our eternity, and we want others to receive God's blessings for themselves. We hear Jesus clearly when he says: *"What does it profit a man to gain the whole world but lose his own soul?"[4]* (Matt. 16:26). But we also feel the challenge of our current context, so despite our commitment to the importance of evangelism, most American Christians feel they do not know how to share the gospel effectively in our culture. It is true, we are in a challenging, less-receptive culture, as missionaries returning to the United States often remind us. But even in this challenging context, there are still great opportunities to help others come to Christ, if we learn how best to engage our culture with the gospel.

Using This Book

This book can be used for Bible classes, small group studies, or personal reading. Each chapter ends with discussion questions and personal reflection questions, which are designed for meaningful reflection and application, both in group settings and individual reading. If you are using this book to teach a class or lead a small group, the discussion questions should be especially helpful, and I suggest asking them at appropriate times throughout your presentation of the material, not just at the end. As for age ranges, this book is suitable for adults, young adults, or college-age.

I look forward to our study over the next thirteen chapters, and I pray God will use it to help us be more effective in sharing the gospel, to his glory.

Endnotes for Introduction

[1] Jim Davis, Michael Graham, Ryan P. Burge, *The Great Dechurching: Who's Leaving, Why Are They Going, and What Will It Take to Bring Them Back?* (Grand Rapids, MI: Zondervan, 2023), 3-5.

[2] Paul W. Chilcote and Laceye C. Warner, editors, *The Study of Evangelism: Exploring a Missional Practice of the Church* (Grand Rapids, MI: Eerdmans, 2008), xx.

[3] A natural question is, "How did you decide what themes would count as a 'post-Christian' evangelism theme?" When I noticed a recurring theme in recent evangelism literature, I measured it against four criteria. If it met all four criteria, I considered it to be part of "post-Christian" evangelism principles. Here are the four-part criteria:
(1) The concept had to be presented as an important factor in a "research-based" discussion of modern-day evangelism.
(2) The concept also had to be presented as an important factor in practical, popular-level evangelism discussions, demonstrating that practical Christian experiences resonated with the research findings.
(3) The concept had to be presented as a shift in thought, emphasis, or practice when compared to past methods of evangelism.
(4) The concept had to be consistent with biblical teaching, to the best of my understanding.

[4] All Scripture references in this book are from the 1995 New American Standard Bible unless otherwise noted.

SECTION ONE:

The Challenge of Post-Christian Culture...and the Way Forward

Chapters 1-2

Chapter 1

The Challenge of
Post-Christian Culture:

Keeping a Bigger Perspective

"For I, the Lord, do not change."—Malachi 3:6

"'Is not My word like fire?' declares the Lord, 'and like a hammer which shatters a rock?'"—Jeremiah 23:29

The World-Changing Gospel

Jesus Christ changed the world forever. Beginning in the small Roman province of Judea, the message about Jesus' life, death, and resurrection lit a fire that has been spreading around the world ever since. The book of Acts describes how the good news of salvation in Jesus spread through the culturally diverse Roman Empire, highlighting the world-changing aspect of the gospel.

The gospel's rapid spread in Acts is a good place to begin a study on evangelism. In the first chapter, Jesus tells his apostles that they will receive God's power through the Holy Spirit and then take the gospel all over the world:

> *"But you will receive power when the Holy Spirit has come upon you; and you shall be My witnesses both in Jerusalem, and in all Judea and Samaria, and even to the remotest part of the earth."*—Acts 1:8

Acts 1:8 serves as an outline for the rest of Acts, because from this point forward, the gospel spreads just as Jesus said it would: in Jerusalem, to Judea and Samaria, and then all over the Roman Empire.

First, the gospel spreads in Jerusalem. In Acts 2, the Holy Spirit comes upon the apostles, Peter preaches to the Jerusalem crowd, and three thousand people are baptized (vv. 37-42). Acts 2:47 then says that people were continually coming to Christ: *"And the Lord was adding to their number day by day those who were being saved."* By the time we reach Acts 4, there are about five thousand male Christians (v. 4), plus who knows how many thousands of female Christians.

After Acts 4, we are not given specific numbers, but the gospel continues to spread in Jerusalem:

> *And all the more believers in the Lord, multitudes of men and women were constantly added to their number.*—Acts 5:14

> *The word of God kept on spreading; and the number of the disciples continued to increase greatly in Jerusalem, and a great many of the priests were becoming obedient to the faith.*
> —Acts 6:7

Next, the gospel spreads to all Judea and Samaria. In Acts 8, persecution begins against Christians in Jerusalem, and the disciples "were all scattered throughout the regions of Judea and Samaria" (v. 1). Verse 4 shows their commitment to God's word as they traveled: *"Therefore, those who had been scattered went about preaching the word."* Acts 8 focuses on one of those scattered Christians: a man named Philip teaching the gospel in Samaria, where many people believe and are baptized (v. 12). Two of the apostles, Peter and John, come to help Philip teach in Samaria, and then they preach the gospel "to many villages of the Samaritans" (Acts 8:25). Just as Jesus foretold in Acts 1:8, the gospel has now spread through Jerusalem (chapters 1 through 7) and to Judea and Samaria in chapter 8.

Then, the gospel spreads to the Gentiles and throughout the Roman Empire. God dramatically teaches Peter that Gentiles can also be Christians, leading to the baptism of Cornelius and his household (Acts 10-11). Scattered Christians also bring the gospel to the multi-ethnic city of Antioch, teaching both Jews and Gentiles (Acts 11:19-20) with great success:

And the hand of the Lord was with them, and a large number who believed turned to the Lord. —Acts 11:21

A few verses later, the growth in Antioch continued: *"And considerable numbers were brought to the Lord."* —Acts 11:24

As the Antioch church grows, God instructs them to send Paul and Barnabas on missionary journeys, beginning in Acts 13. Despite constant opposition, Paul and Barnabas see people come to faith in Christ wherever they go. Churches are established in cities all over the north Mediterranean regions. By midway through Paul's second missionary journey, in Acts 17:6, Romans describe Christians as those "who have upset the world," or those who have "turned the world upside down" (KJV). The gospel had already turned the world upside down less than one generation after the death of Jesus. Just as Jesus foretold in Acts 1:8—*in Jerusalem, and in all Judea and Samaria, and even to the remotest part of the earth.*

In the years after the apostles died, the gospel continued to spread. After all, we did not become Christians by accident. God's word eventually came to our side of the world, someone shared it with us, and we were baptized into Christ like so many untold numbers of people before us. It has been two thousand years since Christ lived on earth, and the gospel continues to change lives everywhere it goes.

The Challenge of Post-Christian Evangelism

The book of Acts is extremely faith-building, reminding us that God works through his message and his people to change the world. And we need the reminder, because reading Acts also brings a sobering reality to mind: I have seen many people become Christians, and I am thankful for every one of them, but I have never personally witnessed the type of evangelistic growth we see in Acts. We occasionally hear of rapid Christian growth in other parts of the world—India, China, Africa, South America—but if you have lived in the United States your entire life, at least in the last few generations, you may feel that rapid Christian growth is rare.

Christians in America are more likely to feel as if fewer people are trying to live for Christ and, sadly, the statistics bear this out. The number of professing Christians has declined significantly over the last fifty years: in 2024, 62% of Americans identified as Christians; that number was 90% in 1972, within living memory of our older generations.[1] Scholars tell us that after decades of growth, most American denominations began a continuous trend of losing members in the mid-1960s.[2] In churches of Christ, our growth continued, albeit slowly, until the early 1990s, when our numbers began declining.[3] But the decline has been noticeable for us too: the number of Americans identifying with churches of Christ dropped 13.4% from 2000-2020.[4]

Historically, American religious movements had been stories of revivalism. Examples include the First and Second Great Awakenings, in which large numbers of people committed themselves to Christianity and thereby shaped a Christian-focused cultural landscape.[5] In contemporary times, one study declared that the last three decades have witnessed the largest religious movement in the history of our country; but this has been a movement *away* from church, as 40 million Americans moved into the "dechurched" category over the past thirty years. [6] The "dechurched" descriptor means that those 40 million once attended church services at least semi-regularly, but no longer attend. The statistics are consistent: modern American culture has far fewer people professing Christianity than past generations.

Those statistics are not surprising, considering that American Christians have undoubtedly felt cultural influences pushing against our faith. Several cultural factors have made Christianity less popular in our country, including:

- Our American **hyper-individualism** shows itself as selfishness and arrogance more than it did in the mid-1900s;[7] and a culture that says "it is all about me" does not fit comfortably with the Christian message of self-sacrifice and putting others above ourselves.

- Our national **wealth** has not helped our faith. America has the greatest number of millionaires and billionaires in the world, and collectively American citizens have 31% of the entire world's money and net worth.[8] The Bible is clear that people can be both wealthy and faithful (Abraham and Job are two such examples), but the Bible is also clear that wealth presents unique temptations that make faith more difficult, including temptations of arrogance and pursuing money more than God. (Some passages to notice: Proverbs 30:8-9; Matthew 6:19-24; 19:23, 1 Timothy 6:6-10, 17-19.)

- There has been a **strong push in our culture toward secularism**,[9] the belief that religion should not play a role in government, education, or other public parts of society.[10] Our older generations remember what for them was a watershed moment when public prayer was no longer allowed in schools. That began a common feature of American culture in the past few decades: lawsuits and secular pressure to push religion—especially Christianity—out of public spaces such as schools, ballgames, and workplaces. The secular mindset wants to confine Christianity to the private sphere, giving many the impression that it is irrelevant, unnecessary, or untrue, and that it is inappropriate to make public affirmations of our faith.

- Our culture has developed **strong negative perceptions of Christianity** in recent decades.[11] These perceptions have been developed in several ways, including:
  - ✓ consistent negative media portrayals of Christians, as hypocritical, ignorant, or worse;
  - ✓ outspoken critics of Christianity who claim that religion is not only wrong, but also hurts society and should not be tolerated;[12]
  - ✓ a push for LGBTQ+ activism, often claiming that Christian convictions about sexual ethics are somehow harmful to those who pursue other sexual lifestyles;
  - ✓ a perception that many Christians are too focused on political agendas, prioritizing political victories above caring for people;[13]
  - ✓ bad examples of people who claim to be Christians (which unfortunately contribute to the negative media portrayals mentioned above)—including popular televangelists found to be hypocrites, sexual abuse scandals connected to churches, or people having personal bad experiences with Christians. Sadly, a common feature of recent American culture has been "bad church experience" stories, which have resulted in many disengaging from Christianity.[14]

With a declining number of people professing Christianity and a culture actively pushing against it, many scholars now describe American culture as "post-Christian." What do they mean by "post-Christian"? The term simply means that Christianity is no longer the dominant cultural influence in our country that it once was. The same term is applied to countries in the European and Australian regions that have experienced similar cultural trajectories. Whether you think "post-Christian" is an appropriate label or not,[15] it is the descriptor commonly applied today for cultures like ours, so we will stay consistent with current practice and use it in this book as well. Scholar David Gustafson explains why America has been increasingly considered a post-Christian culture:

> A growing percentage of Americans no longer share a
> Christian worldview, hold to Christian beliefs and values, or
> identify with America's Christian heritage. The Christian faith
> no longer has the cultural clout of previous decades, nor can
> one assume that people are familiar with Christian theological
> concepts like sin, faith, prayer, repentance, and a personal God.
> Indeed, these are (mis)understood as bad deeds, wishful
> thinking, meditation, moral expectations, and a moldable
> deity.[16]

In the term "post"-Christian, you also notice the implication that we are not "pre"-Christian, and thus our culture is different from those that have never encountered Christianity. While "pre-Christian" cultures hear the Christian message for the first time, often appreciating its values and respecting its followers, people in "post-Christian" culture often begin with preconceived notions *against* Christianity, even before they are exposed to genuine Christian faith. Again, Gustafson summarizes the situation well:

> Those living in post-Christendom contexts may know very
> little of the Christian faith but assume they know more than
> they do. Their limited perceptions inoculate them against
> biblical Christianity. ... In the end, many see the Christian

faith, or a caricature of it, as something they already know and to be rejected.[17]

The Way Forward: Seeking a Bigger Perspective

Should we just give up? After witnessing the spiritual decline of recent decades, Christians might feel discouraged, tempted to believe that the gospel no longer has a place in our culture. If we have adopted that mindset, consciously or subconsciously, then it is time to renew our evangelism convictions.

Rebuilding those convictions is a central goal of these opening chapters. To meet our current cultural moment, Christians must develop a more positive evangelism mindset. Now is the time to renew our confidence in the power of the gospel and our commitment to sharing it. When Christians understand what is possible and remember why it matters, they are empowered to move forward in faith. As we begin this study, it is important to identify our culture's evangelism challenges, but it is also important to rekindle our evangelism convictions.

For the remainder of this first chapter, we offer a good first step forward: seeking a bigger perspective, not just on our challenges, but also on our faith. It is easy to focus on the spiritually frustrating direction of our culture. But before we get stuck obsessing over the obstacles, here are a few faith reminders about the possibilities for the path ahead:

First, the same God is still leading his church.

God made promises about his church. In Daniel 2:44, God promised his kingdom would never be destroyed, would outlast all other kingdoms, and would endure forever. In Matthew 16:18, Jesus told his apostles that he was building his church—the church was God's idea! —and that the gates of Hades itself could not overpower it. God also made promises about his presence: *"I am with you always, even to the end of the age"* (Matt. 28:20).

Before getting too concerned about the challenges facing Christians in American culture, remember who God is. This is the one true God, who keeps his promises. This is the God who led Israel out from Egypt, giving them victory over the most powerful nation then on earth. This is the God who led that small group of apostles to change the world. As Paul said in Romans 8:31, *"If God is for us, who is against us?"* God is all-powerful, and we are with him.

God has also shown an ability to turn circumstances around when people least expect it. The Egyptian army had the Israelites cornered, and then God parted the Red Sea and gave his people a most improbable victory. Jesus died and it appeared evil had won, and then Jesus raised from the dead and showed the true meaning of the cross and the power of God.

With God's track record of turning circumstances around, it may be unwise to assume that our culture will drift hopelessly away from God. We do not know God's plans, but we know God's history of changing circumstances in ways people did not expect. In fact, we have seen him do it in our own country's history. In 1822, Thomas Jefferson predicted, "There is not a young man now living in the U.S. who will not die a Unitarian."[18] What did he mean by that? Jefferson believed the religious trajectory of the country was turning against belief in the Bible's miracles and doctrines such as the divinity of Jesus, and he thought true New Testament Christianity would simply fade away, replaced by a form of religion more acceptable to the secular mindset. Little did Jefferson know, the seeds were already growing for one of our nation's largest-ever religious revivals. It would become known as the Second Great Awakening, and it produced a strong movement back toward God and the Bible. Notably for those of us in churches of Christ, the Second Great Awakening included the Restoration Movement. The Restoration Movement proclaimed a return to the teachings of the New Testament, rejecting man-made teachings and seeking Christian unity based on apostolic practices, a message that led to many churches of Christ being established in America. While it looked to

Jefferson and others as if biblical faith was on the way out, God had something completely different in mind.

A similar story could be told about American faith in the early 1900s. Atheism was growing and becoming more outspoken, and it was commonly predicted that Christianity would disappear as science and technology kept advancing. [19] Then came World War I, the Great Depression, and World War II, and out of those events grew perhaps the most faith-oriented generation our country has ever seen. (The one in which 90% professed Christianity, as mentioned earlier.)

We do not know the future, but we know God has a way of turning circumstances around when people least expect it. Therefore, Christians should not lose hope and assume our culture is a lost cause—God may have something in mind. We have seen him arrange conditions that led to revival in the 1800s and the 1900s. Who knows what God has in mind for the 2000s? And whether a revival of faith happens or not, God promises his church will endure and he will still be with his people, providing guidance and strength. As we engage a challenging culture, may we not forget the power and promises of God.

Second, the gospel is still powerful and continues to change lives.

Christians have always loved Paul's words in Romans 1:16:

For I am not ashamed of the gospel, for it is the power of God for salvation to everyone who believes, to the Jew first and also to the Greek.

The gospel is God's power for salvation! Gospel means "good news," referring to the message of what God has done in Jesus Christ. Mark 1:1 introduces the entire book of Mark as the "gospel of Jesus Christ, the Son of God." The gospel therefore includes Jesus' life, miracles, teachings, sacrificial death, resurrection, enthronement at the right hand of the Father, establishment of his church as an all-nations people of God, and promise to return for final judgment and eternal rewards.

As Paul spoke about the gospel in 1 Corinthians 15:1-4, he reminded the Corinthians that the gospel is how "you are saved" (v. 2), and he reaffirmed what is "of first importance" in the gospel message:

> *For I delivered to you as of first importance what I also received, that Christ died for our sins according to the Scriptures, and that He was buried, and that He was raised on the third day according to the Scriptures.* —1 Corinthians 15:3-4

The message of Jesus is powerful. It brings salvation and changes lives everywhere it goes. As Christians today, we are living proof of the gospel's ongoing impact. We heard the gospel, it convicted our hearts, and we made the commitment to be baptized into Christ, rising to walk in new life for him. Many others continue to do the same, around the world and in America as well. Every culture brings unique challenges, but the gospel is still powerful, and it changes lives wherever it goes. As we engage our challenging culture, may we not forget the power of the gospel.

Third, the gospel has flourished in challenging contexts before.

Although America is not "pre-Christian" like the first-century Roman Empire, it is helpful to remember that the early church faced cultural challenges also,[20] and yet the gospel flourished. The Roman Empire was an extremely diverse religious world, with a variety of religions, idols, cults, and philosophies. Sinful sexual lifestyles were commonplace, including homosexuality, prostitution, and a broad acceptance of adultery. The Roman Empire also developed strong undercurrents of disdain toward Christianity, from both Jews and Romans, leading to ostracism and persecution of believers. Those challenges were the cultural background for the book of Acts, and yet as we saw at the beginning of this chapter, the gospel still spread rapidly. The first-century challenges remind us that, in many ways, God's people have been here before.

Christianity has engaged difficult contexts many times over the past two thousand years, and yet it continues to grow. In fact, despite the global influence of post-Christian countries like America, it is encouraging to know that Christianity continues to multiply worldwide. Recent projections from Pew Research Center predict that while the secularization of America will likely continue over the coming decades, the global number of professing Christians is expected to keep growing, maintaining over 31% of the world's population between now and 2050 even as the world's population is projected to grow significantly.[21] Another Pew Research projection looked even further out, predicting that professing Christians will rise closer to 32% of world population by 2060, again even with an expected significant increase in world population.[22] Those studies also project that people claiming "no religion" will shrink from 16% to 13% of the world's population. As those projections show, the world is expected to become more religious and more Christian in the next few decades, not less. Sometimes we get tunnel vision in our own culture and forget that the gospel continues to spread around the world.

Despite the challenges, there is nothing about our culture that makes it impossible for the gospel to change lives and spread successfully here as well. Every culture has challenges and false stories that compete against God's truth—that reality began with the serpent's lie in the Garden of Eden, and it will continue until Christ's return. In that sense, our culture is no different than every other culture that hears the gospel, so Christians must seek to understand our context and adjust. As we engage our challenging culture, may we remember that Christianity has faced many challenging cultures over the past two thousand years, and yet it continues to flourish. It continues to change lives around the world today, and there is no reason it cannot flourish in our own culture as well.

The Way Forward: Thinking Like Missionaries

Yes, our culture has become a challenging one for sharing the gospel, as missionaries returning to America often remind us. But instead of focusing solely on the challenges, may we also see what is possible, based on our trust in the power of God and the gospel. That is a great first step as we prepare to share the gospel with those around us.

In fact, that is the first step Christian missionaries have been taking for two thousand years. With a deep trust that God will bless their efforts, they commit themselves to share the gospel in a particular cultural context. Then they prepare by studying that culture, seeking to understand how best to evangelize among that group of people. They often ask certain questions:

- How much does this culture know about Christianity?
- What do they think about Christianity, and what questions do they have?
- How direct can we be with people in this culture?
- What holds people back from becoming Christians in this culture?
- What cultural characteristics provide open doors for the gospel, and how can we connect with those?

After studying those questions, missionaries go forward in faith, with a better understanding of how best to share the gospel with that culture and trusting God to provide the increase.

Recognizing that our culture has changed, American Christians must learn to follow their example and think like missionaries for our own context.[23] With a deep trust in God and his word, we want to ask: how can we share the gospel more effectively in this increasingly post-Christian culture? That is the overarching question of this book, and every chapter is intended to provide helpful insights and answers.

It is fair to ask, where do these answers come from? This book brings together key themes from the many evangelism writings of the past few decades, distilling the best concepts and practices into a set of *post-Christian evangelism principles*. These are principles that Christians have found to be effective for sharing the gospel in our cultural context; and most importantly, they are all firmly rooted in Scripture. (For more on the core question behind this book and how it originated, be sure to read the introduction section.)

We want to start thinking like missionaries, reexamining how to evangelize effectively in our challenging culture.

Here is an overview of the post-Christian evangelism principles we will explore in this book:

- Evangelism Perspective
- Evangelistic Prayer
- Evangelistic Patience
- Evangelism Personalities
- Evangelistic Motives
- Evangelism Pathways
- Evangelism and Faith Conversations
- Evangelistic Church Cultures
- Evangelistic Bible Studies

By the time we are finished, those concepts will have greater meaning, and we should feel better equipped than ever before to engage our culture with the gospel.

These first two chapters are intended to address the first item on that list, building a more positive *evangelism perspective*, which has become more difficult for Christians as our culture has become less receptive. In this chapter, we introduced some of our culture's faith challenges, but we reminded ourselves to keep a *bigger perspective* on God and the gospel, helping us move forward in faith that great things are always possible with God. In the next chapter, we will discuss the "evangelism crisis" among Christians in post-Christian culture, and we will reaffirm our own foundational commitment to evangelism. After all, if we want to move forward with a more positive mindset about evangelism, we must make sure we have the right foundations.

Discussion Questions

1) What factors made the gospel spread so rapidly in the first century, as recorded in the book of Acts?

2) Have you noticed a decrease of Christian faith in our culture during your lifetime? In what ways have you seen it?

3) What makes evangelism difficult in our current American culture?

4) What do people mean when they describe a culture as "post-Christian"?

5) How is our "post-Christian" culture different from a "pre-Christian" culture?

6) Do you agree that God can turn cultures around quickly? Can you give some examples of God turning circumstances around, whether in the Bible or in more recent history?

7) What is the gospel? What makes it so life-changing, no matter the culture?

8) Do you think every culture has challenges for evangelism? What challenges in the first-century Roman Empire made evangelism difficult for the early church?

9) How do foreign missionaries prepare to travel to a new culture and share the gospel? What can we learn from their thought process about how to engage our own changing culture?

10) Do you think Christians struggle to be hopeful about sharing the gospel in our culture? What thoughts from this chapter help change our mindset in a more positive direction?

Personal Reflection

1) Have I allowed the secularism push in our culture to affect me? Am I tempted to hide my Christian faith instead of sharing it? Why?

2) Have I allowed myself to think that the gospel cannot or will not spread in our culture? If so, what can I remember from this chapter to help turn my thinking around?

3) How did I become a Christian? What helped me listen to God instead of listening to our culture? How can I help others grow toward that same conviction?

Endnotes for Chapter 1

[1] The 2024 statistics from:

Pew Research Center. 2025. "2023-24 U.S. Religious Landscape Study Interactive Database." doi: 10.58094/3zs9-jc14. March 2025. https://www.pewresearch.org/religious-landscape-study/

The 1972 statistics from:

Pew Research Center, "Modeling the Future of Religion in America," September 13, 2022. https://www.pewresearch.org/religion/2022/09/13/modeling-the-future-of-religion-in-america/

[2] Gil Rendle, *Quietly Courageous* (Lanham, MD: Rowman and Littlefield, 2019), 19-21.

[3] *Churches of Christ in the United States*, historical data compiled by Carl Royster (Nashville, TN: 21st Century Christian, 2018), 22.

[4] *Churches of Christ in the United States.* The 2020 statistics listed at https://www.21stcc.com/pdfs/ccusa_stats_sheet.pdf.

[5] The First and Second "Great Awakenings" were religious movements in the early United States, producing revival of committed Christian faith and numerous conversions to Christianity. The "Great Awakening" (we now call it the "first" one) took place in the New England and middle American colonies, from about 1720-1750, although the dates vary by source and how you define the movement. The "Second Great Awakening" took place in what was by then the new American nation, approximately during the 1790s through the 1830s.

[6] Jim Davis, Michael Graham, Ryan P. Burge. *The Great Dechurching: Who's Leaving, Why Are They Going, and What Will It Take to Bring Them Back?* (Grand Rapids, MI: Zondervan, 2023), 3-5.

[7] Rendle, *Quietly Courageous*, 23-24.

[8] "How Rich Are Americans on a Global Scale? Very Rich!" SportofMoney.com, October 31, 2022. https://www.sportofmoney.com/how-rich-are-americans-on-a-global-scale-very-rich/

[9] Brittanica.com definition for secularism.

[10] Barna Group, *Reviving Evangelism: Current Realities that Demand a New Vision for Sharing Faith* (Ventura, CA: Barna Group, 2019), 88-89.

[11] Barna Group, *Reviving Evangelism*, 88-89.

[12] Such as the so-called "New Atheism" authors of the early 2000s.

[13] David Kinnaman and Gabe Lyons, *unChristian: What a New Generation Really Thinks About* Christianity (Grand Rapids, MI: Baker Books, 2007), 153-171.

[14] Kinnaman and Lyons, *unchristian*, 31-32.

[15] I confess that I have come to dislike the term "post-Christian." If I were to describe our culture, it seems to me we are a "secularizing" culture, although that descriptor does not capture people's attention like "post-Christian" does. I do not think the term post-Christian is wrong, per se, but it tends to carry connotations with which I disagree. The term might suggest that Christianity is somehow outdated or disappearing, neither of which I believe. The Bible promises that God's kingdom will never be destroyed (Daniel 2:44), and that

even the gates of Hades cannot overpower it (Matthew 16:18). So, I am not an alarmist who believes Christianity will cease to exist in America. In fact, I am very hopeful about the future of Christianity in our country, as this book—and even this chapter—will make clear.

My friend Matt Mitchell also dislikes the term "post-Christian" because it might imply a "perfectly-Christian" time that preceded the post-Christian period we are currently in. As we noted earlier in this chapter, even in those generations when more Americans professed Christianity, there were still many poor examples that did not live up to true Christian teachings. As Matt says it: "Many can remember American life in the mid-20ᵗʰ century when Christian morality, motifs, acceptance, and conversations were public and present. We must remember, though, the wisdom from Solomon in Ecclesiastes 7:10. The good old days were not always good for everyone. Let us not think, therefore, that American cultural periods of the past did not struggle with issues that were markedly un-Christian (racial segregation, for example)." (Personal email correspondence, May 13, 2025, used with permission.)

Despite our quibbles, the term post-Christian is what many use to describe a culture that is no longer "pre-Christian" and is also no longer dominated by Christian ideas like it once was. Thus, we are using post-Christian in this book, to be consistent with the common practice, and with the hope that no one will get the impression that using the term means I think Christianity is disappearing or that I think past generations in America were perfect, because I do not.

[16] David M. Gustafson, *Gospel Witness: Evangelism in Word and Deed* (Grand Rapids, MI: Eerdmans, 2019), 3. See his broader description of post-Christian culture on pages 2-7.

[17] Gustafson, *Gospel Witness*, 5.

[18] Thomas Jefferson, "1822 Letter to Dr. Benjamin Waterhouse." June 26, 1822. (As some sources explain, Jefferson meant, at least, that they would not be a "Trinitarian.") https://founders.archives.gov/documents/Jefferson/03-18-02-0437.

[19] As noted, for example, in summaries like this one: "In the late 19th century, an array of celebrity philosophers—the likes of Friedrich Nietzsche, Karl Marx, and Sigmund Freud—proclaimed the death of God, and predicted that atheism would follow scientific discovery and modernity in the West, sure as smoke follows fire." Derek Thompson, "Three Decades Ago, America Lost Its Religion. Why?" *The Atlantic,* September 26, 2019.

[20] For a deeper study of the challenges, see Michael Green, *Evangelism in the Early Church*, revised edition (Grand Rapids, MI: Eerdmans, 2003), chapter 2 "Obstacles to Evangelism," 50-75.

[21] "Key Findings from the Global Religious Futures Project," December 21, 2022. Pew Research Center. www.pewresearch.org.

[22] "The Changing Global Religious Landscape," Pew Research Center, April 5, 2017. www.pewresearch.org.

[23] This concept of reframing our culture as a mission field and thinking like missionaries is found in several recent evangelism resources, including Michael Frost and Alan Hirsch, *The Shaping of Things to Come: Innovation and Mission for the 21ˢᵗ Century Church*, Revised and updated edition (Baker Books, 2013).

Chapter 2

The Challenge of
Post-Christian Culture:

Rebuilding Our Evangelism
Foundations

*"For I am not ashamed of the gospel, for it is the power of God for
salvation to everyone who believes, to the Jew first and also to the Greek."*
—Romans 1:16

The Post-Christian Evangelism Crisis

It is important for Christians to understand the evangelism challenges in our increasingly post-Christian culture. But to meet our cultural moment, Christians must learn to think bigger than the challenges, rekindling our evangelism convictions and regaining a more positive perspective on evangelism. In the first chapter, we acknowledged that our culture has been drifting away from Christianity; but we reminded ourselves of the power of God and the life-changing nature of the gospel.

In this chapter, we want to address another significant problem in post-Christian culture: American Christians have become less and less active in evangelism. Several recent studies identify this issue:

- In a 2017 Barna study, more than one thousand American churchgoers were given a list of Christian activities, and they ranked them according to which activities they most enjoyed. When the results were collected, evangelism ranked last.[1]

- A 2018 Barna study found that "Christians are among the most likely to feel tension" in conversations with people who believe differently.[2] If Christians are among the most likely to feel tension in conversations that involve differences, it makes sense that Christians tend to avoid those conversations.

- A 2019 Barna Research report on evangelism found that nearly half of practicing Christians in the millennial generation (47%) said it is wrong to evangelize.[3] Did these millennials misunderstand what was meant by evangelism, or are they questioning whether it is morally wrong to evangelize?

- That same 2019 report found that 56% of Christians had only two or fewer conversations about faith with a non-Christian during the previous year.[4]

Seeing those statistics, it is not surprising that the 2019 Barna report summarized their research findings by stating: "U.S. Christians are losing a desire to share their faith."[5]

Do those statistics resonate with you? Do you feel uneasy about sharing your faith in our culture? It is reasonable to assume that many Christians do, at least to some extent. After all, the cultural challenges we discussed in Chapter One are real. Given the negative portrayal of Christianity in today's culture, it is understandable to feel hesitant about expressing or sharing our faith.

Christians on short-term mission trips often find it easier to share their faith abroad than at home. They meet people who are receptive, they do not worry that someone might get mad at them, and they do not fear negative consequences for discussing their faith. Some of this can be attributed to the renewed sense of spiritual commitment often present during a mission trip, or to the reality that being far from home, there is less risk of negative consequences in our day-to-day relationships. But another reason for those feelings is the recognition that American culture is less receptive, and sometimes even hostile, to certain methods of evangelism.

In our less-receptive culture, it is easy to understand why Christians get discouraged. We occasionally have bad evangelism experiences, tempting us to avoid the practice altogether in the future. For example, one writer reflected on a disappointing summer of door-to-door evangelism in London, England (another post-Christian culture). After months of rejection and no positive responses, he decided evangelism must not be his talent, and he came home ready to quit evangelism for good.[6] Even if our experiences are not that extreme, we feel the social tension against discussing faith in our culture. One study noted that America has developed a secular social code that tends to discourage evangelistic conversations: Americans think "people should not criticize someone else's life choices" and "people can believe whatever they want as long as those beliefs don't affect society."[7] With that type of social expectation, some individuals consider it inappropriate or even offensive for Christians to share their faith, and Christians are wary of that social tension. In these ways and others, our secular culture discourages evangelism, leaving some Christians with bad experiences from trying, and leaving all of us feeling the pressure to make it less of a priority.

If it is true that Christians are feeling pressure to hide their faith, I pray God will help us overcome that temptation, because both Scripture and modern evangelism studies agree on this crucial point: for evangelism to be most effective, it requires individual Christian involvement. It cannot rely exclusively on the Sunday sermons or professional ministers, nor can it depend on mass marketing or advertising. In the book of Acts, the gospel spread through the apostles' teaching, but it also spread because many individual Christians shared the gospel everywhere they went, even when they were being persecuted for their faith (see Acts 8:1-4). That principle is still true today. As we will see in statistics later in this book, the most common way someone becomes a Christian is through a personal relationship with a Christian. We need more individual Christians engaged in the evangelism process, encouraging the non-Christians in their life!

It is especially interesting to see this principle highlighted by one church that initially tried a different approach. This church decided to make their worship services more entertainment-oriented, thinking that entertainment would appeal to American unbelievers and bring them to Christ. The church later did a self-study of their results and concluded that the best way to evangelize was not through changing worship into an entertainment atmosphere. Instead, they declared that "the most effective outreach strategy—bar none" is motivating individual Christ-centered members to engage in evangelism.[8] That principle has been found true over and over: individual Christian involvement is essential for effective evangelism.

In summary, this is the current evangelism crisis in our country: individual Christian involvement is essential for effective evangelism, yet many Christians feel hesitant to be part of it. If our less-receptive, post-Christian culture has indeed made us less excited about sharing our faith, how can we get moving again? Consider three things to help rebuild our commitment to evangelism:

Rebuilding Our Evangelism Foundations: Aligning Our Heart with God's Heart

First, Christians should desire to align our hearts with God's, and God cares deeply about bringing souls back to him. One way to know what God cares about is to see what he emphasizes in Scripture. The Bible gives the real story of the world, and it is a story of God reaching out to humanity, seeking to restore the relationship that is lost when we choose sin. To highlight this emphasis, notice four major sections in the big-picture story of Scripture, and how God's desire for human salvation stands at the forefront of each:

1) <u>Early Chapters of Genesis</u> – As the Bible begins, God creates everything "good," and gives humanity true choice whether to follow him or not. Adam and Eve's sin separates them from God and the blessings of fellowship with him. Sin has consequences, yet God continues to love them, clothing them with garments, helping them give birth to a new generation, and continuing communication with their family regarding how to be in fellowship with him.

2) <u>Old Testament Covenants</u> – Through the Old Testament covenants—such as the ones with Noah, Abraham, and the Israelites—God shows the world the blessing of being in a covenant relationship with him, in contrast to the devastating effects of sin. God builds a covenant people in the Israelites, showing both his judgment on sin and his merciful forgiveness. He promises a day when all nations will be blessed through Abraham's people (Gen. 12:1-3), in a kingdom made up of people from every nation (Dan. 7:13-14).

3) <u>The Life of Jesus</u> – God's Son comes to earth "to seek and save the lost" (Luke 19:10), and he shows God's love and wisdom through his life, healings, and teachings. His death on the cross to atone for humanity's sins is the clearest expression of God's love and desire for relationship with us. His resurrection shows that he is truly God and still reigns over his creation, and that through him we also can have eternal life.

4) <u>The Mission of the Church</u> – Jesus hands his mission to the church, which is a theme emphasized at the end of all four gospel accounts, including what is often called "The Great Commission" (Matt. 28:18-20).

In the book of Acts, God works through his church to help the gospel spread, bringing salvation to people of all nations. The church is tasked with sharing the gospel to the lost until Christ returns.

In those four "acts" of Scripture, we see the world's true story: sin separates humanity from God, yet God continues to reach out, giving us the opportunity to restore our relationship with him. God cares deeply about reaching out with the message of salvation!

Within that big-picture story of the Bible, many individual passages highlight that God's heart is in evangelism. These truths have kindled an evangelistic spirit within Christians for two thousand years, and it might be worth memorizing some of them to regularly remind ourselves of the importance of evangelism. Scripture tells us:

- God wants all people to be saved (1 Tim. 2:4).
- Heaven rejoices at every soul that comes back to God (Luke 15:7,10).
- Jesus described God as the prodigal son's father, waiting hopefully for his child to come back home, running to meet his son as he comes back, and wishing that all his children had the same love for lost souls (Luke 15:11-32).
- God shows the depths of his love by dying for us, not when we were worthy but when we were sinners (Rom. 5:8).
- Jesus felt compassion as he saw the lost multitudes and he longed for more of God's people to help souls come back to God (Matt. 9:36-38).
- Jesus taught that one soul is worth more than the entire world (Matt. 16:26).

Passages like these show us the importance of souls and salvation in the eyes of God, and they challenge us to deepen our own love for souls.

Christians should care about what God cares about, and God's heart is in evangelism. Heaven rejoiced when you and I came back to God through

Christ. God hopes other souls will make that same decision. As we rebuild our evangelistic foundations, we must remember how much God cares about souls and rekindle a desire to align our hearts with his.

Rebuilding Our Evangelism Foundations: Committed to Evangelism

Second, after rekindling our heart for God's evangelistic mission, we must commit ourselves to participating in that mission. Evangelism participation requires time and effort, which we sometimes struggle to give. People often focus solely on their own activities, filling their schedules with busyness and personal goals. However, we must not allow God's mission to get left out of our lives. Remembering that every soul will stand before God one day in eternity, it is worth any effort to participate in evangelism.

Yet there is a caution to avoid here also: some evangelism writers worry that Christians can develop an unhealthy anxiety about evangelism.[9] Such anxiety grows when Christians feel as if everyone else's salvation depends entirely on them, or that they have failed God if they do not have the perfect answer in every conversation with an unbeliever, or that they are not really pleasing to God unless they have brought someone else to Christ. This mindset incorrectly makes other people's salvation more about our actions than about their choices. And sadly, evangelistic anxiety can cause Christians to interact with unbelievers in inappropriate ways, which often pushes people away from wanting to learn about Christianity.

Here is a concept to set in our minds, a goal that more accurately presents the mindset of Jesus and his followers in the New Testament: *we want to be committed to evangelism without being anxious about it.* That might be worth repeating to ourselves to let it sink in.

How can we be committed to God's evangelistic mission without being anxious about it? Consider both parts of that goal:

We want to be committed to evangelism. Jesus was clear in giving his mission to the church:

> *And Jesus came up and spoke to them, saying, "All authority has been given to Me in heaven and on earth. Go therefore and make disciples of all the nations, baptizing them in the name of the Father and the Son and the Holy Spirit, teaching them to observe all that I commanded you; and lo, I am with you always, even to the end of the age."*—Matthew 28:18-20

To whom is Jesus speaking in this passage? In context, he is speaking to the apostles, but the wording suggests he is speaking even beyond the apostles, saying in verse 20: "I am with you always, even to the end of the age." The apostles would not live until the end of the Christian age, so Jesus is not speaking only to them. The "you" in this passage refers to Christ's church, all disciples throughout the Christian age until his return. This passage is for you and me just as it was for the apostles. When we become a follower of Jesus, we join Jesus in his evangelistic mission, and we want to be committed to it.

We want to be committed to evangelism without being anxious about evangelism. We do not want to be anxious about evangelism. Jesus and Paul both cared deeply about people, but they also knew that God gives choice, and every person must make their own decision between themselves and God. When the rich young ruler walked away from Jesus, Jesus allowed him to go, knowing he had to make his own decision regarding his relationship with God (Matt. 19:21-23). Pressuring him or badgering him would not help, he had a personal heart choice he needed to make.

When King Agrippa stated that Paul might soon persuade him to become a Christian, Paul did not try to pressure him; rather, he gave Agrippa a simple encouragement, hoping that both Agrippa and everyone else listening would become Christians (Acts 26:28-29). Paul did not react as if Agrippa's salvation depended on Paul; Paul simply shared the gospel and hoped his listeners would decide to follow it. Paul knew Agrippa had his own decision to make between himself and God. That is how Jesus or Paul handled evangelism: they shared the gospel and encouraged people to follow it, but they also allowed people to make their own decisions, even if they walked away.

We must remember that people are responsible for their own choices and actions. In Romans 1:18-21, Paul writes that every person can see in creation that there is a God we should be seeking, and thus we are all "without excuse" (v. 20). If someone is not seeking God, that is a choice they are making. Their choice is not my fault or my responsibility. Sometimes we wish we could make other people's decisions for them, but that's not how God-given freedom of choice works. We can encourage people to follow Jesus—and we want to be committed to that—but we must also remember that people are making their own heart choices. If we anxiously take responsibility for someone else's salvation, we are tempted to make their salvation more about us than about them. This might lead us to pressure people inappropriately or badger them in ways that hinder them from recognizing their own responsibility to follow God.

Another look at Matthew 28:18-20 helps us avoid unhealthy anxiety about evangelism, because that passage also teaches that Christ's mission is not mine alone. As we noted above, this passage is for the entire church. The "you" spoken by Jesus is plural in the original Greek, and it refers to all Christians until the end of the age. Christ's mission is not for any single individual alone, or else we would each be required to personally make a disciple of Jesus from every single nation on earth ("make disciples of all the nations"), because that's the only way an individual can fulfill Jesus' command by themselves. This passage is for the church as a corporate body, it is not my responsibility alone. Taking the gospel to all nations is something we do as a church, with all Christians working together to share the gospel. The passage also teaches that Jesus is with us as we carry out this task: *"I am with you always, even to the end of the age."* We must not allow ourselves to feel as if someone else's salvation depends entirely on us, for we are not alone in the task. It is critical to remember that other Christians and God himself will also work in their life to encourage them toward Christ.

We conclude this point by reiterating the proper goal: we want to be committed to evangelism. While someone else's salvation is not my responsibility, it is my responsibility to encourage them to follow Jesus. This book is filled with ways to encourage others in their faith, and those actions will require time, effort, and attention. They will require less focus on ourselves and more focus on others. Sometimes people will respond positively and sometimes they will not. If we are committed to evangelism, we will be willing to make those sacrifices. God wants all Christians to join him in his evangelistic mission—may we recommit ourselves to it.

Rebuilding Our Evangelism Foundations: Getting Over Our Barriers

Third, we want to get over our evangelism barriers. Evangelism barriers are the things that hold us back from participating in God's evangelism mission. They cause us to avoid religious conversations or leave us afraid to give an invitation to a church event.

One study revealed the three most common barriers that keep American Christians from participating in evangelism, and most of us can relate to these fears:[10]

1)   I do not want to be pushy.
2)   I do not feel qualified.
3)   I do not know what to say.

What might we say to someone struggling with those barriers? Since these are the most common, here are some brief thoughts on each:

"I do not want to be pushy." We realize that people in our culture do not like to be pressured, whether the topic is buying a car, getting insurance, or thinking about religion. But who said evangelism should be pushy? This barrier partially comes from the way Christians have thought about evangelism. Evangelism is not about pressuring people to do something they do not want to do. Evangelism is not about inappropriate confrontation, or talking "at" people, or argumentative debating, or manipulation. Again, people have their own decision to make, and we cannot pressure or manipulate anyone into making a sincere heart decision. Evangelism is sharing the gospel and encouraging unbelievers to follow it. I am optimistic enough to believe it is possible to share our faith without being pushy, and when we do that, people will usually respond kindly, even if they do not accept what we say. We must find ways to encourage faith in a non-pressuring manner and not allow a fear of being pushy to hold us back from participating in God's evangelistic mission.

"I do not feel qualified." No one is qualified! Even the apostle Paul said about sharing the gospel: "who is adequate for these things?" (2 Cor. 2:16). One study found that only 1% of professing Christians consider themselves gifted as evangelists.[11] We will not always say the right thing. We will not always know the answer to the question, and we may not even understand the question. That is okay. Remember, this is God's mission, and he is with us in it (Matt. 28:20). God can use even our imperfect evangelistic efforts to produce good things. Throughout Scripture, God used unqualified people to spread his message: Moses, who knew he was not a good speaker (Exod. 4:10-13); the Samaritan woman, who was living a sinful lifestyle (John 4:28-30, 39-42); and the apostles, who everyone knew were not formally educated (Acts 4:13). The list goes on and on. Besides the Lord himself, no one is qualified, but we go forward with the blessing of God, trusting he will cause the growth (1 Cor. 3:6-7). Even if we feel unqualified, we must not allow that feeling to stop us from joining God's evangelistic mission.

"I do not know what to say." It is true, we want to do our best to explain our faith to those who ask (1 Pet. 3:15). But our words will rarely—

if ever—be "perfect." There will always be something we do not know. If we wait to share our faith until we know how to always say the perfect words and give all the perfect answers, none of us will ever share the gospel. If someone has a question we are not sure about, there is nothing wrong with saying, "I don't know, let me look into that and get back with you." The goal is not to win a debate, and the other person must decide whether they are asking an honest question or giving an excuse to avoid faith. Be an encourager: let non-Christians know you would love to have them come to worship or Bible class with you sometime. Let those who have been considering Christianity know you would love to see them be baptized into Christ. Your words will rarely be perfect, but that does not mean you are failing God. Your faith and conversation by itself will stir up others to think about their own faith. We must not allow a fear of imperfect words to hold us back from participating in God's evangelistic mission.

You may have other evangelism barriers besides those three, and it is worth settling our minds on how to get past them. For example, some Christians worry about making relationships awkward by discussing faith. Here is what I tell myself about that worry: I will do my best not to let it be awkward, during or after our faith conversation. I will act normal and kind to the best of my ability, even if I sense the other person feels different around me. If they decide they do not want to be my friend after learning I am a committed Christian, that will be their decision to make, but I still want to show kindness and encourage faith in those around me. Whatever our evangelism barrier, we need to find a mental encouragement to match it and help us overcome it. What barriers do you feel about evangelism? How would you help a fellow Christian get over that barrier?

There are occasions when it is necessary to take risks in relationships and move beyond our comfort zones, which is part of Christian maturity. Therefore, let us commit ourselves to overcoming our evangelism barriers, praying that God would help us, and start playing a bigger part in God's evangelistic mission. Remember, we are all doing this together, and God is with us.

Moving Forward with Renewed Foundations

May we hear the consistent message of these first two chapters: the answer to a challenging culture is not to give up on evangelism. As our culture became less receptive, many Christians shied away from evangelism, fearful of negative responses. Satan wants us to believe that outreach is hopeless or scary so that the gospel will not spread. To avoid that pitfall, we must reflect more deeply on what we believe about God, the gospel, and evangelism.

In these initial chapters, we have shared faith reminders that help us move forward with a *more positive evangelism perspective*: regaining a bigger perspective of God and his life-changing word (as we saw in Chapter One) and renewing our foundational commitment to evangelism (the focus of this chapter).

It is important for Christians to begin with a more positive evangelism perspective; yet sharing our faith demands even more than that. Even if Christians are faithfully committed to God's evangelistic mission, many do not know how to share the gospel in our changing culture. It is to that question we now turn. In the next section, which makes up most of this book, we will present mindset-shifts and action steps that Christians have found to be essential for post-Christian evangelism. What produces effective evangelism in our culture? With faith in an all-powerful God and a renewed commitment to his evangelistic mission, it is time to start answering that question in more detail.

Discussion Questions:

1) Do you think Christians in America have become less involved in evangelism than in previous generations? If so, why might that be happening?

2) Do you agree that the big-picture story of the Bible is God reaching out to sinful humanity with the offer of salvation through a relationship with him? If so, what does that tell us about our biggest need in life and what life is all about?

3) What passages of Scripture tell us about God's love for the lost and his desire that they return to him? Do you have a favorite?

4) Is Matthew 28:18-20 a command for just the apostles or for the entire church until the end of time? How do you know?

5) Is the Matthew 28:18-20 command to take the gospel to all nations a command for you to fulfill by yourself alone, or for the church as a whole? What would it require for one person to fulfill it by themselves? How does it help my evangelistic mindset when I realize that command is for the entire church and not for me alone?

6) Do you agree with the concept of being "committed" to evangelism but trying not to be "anxious" about evangelism? If I feel anxious about someone else's salvation, how might that lead me to act toward them in ways that are not helpful?

7) Am I responsible for someone else's salvation? Why or why not? What are my responsibilities regarding someone else's relationship with God?

8) What are some common barriers that keep Christians from participating in evangelism?

9) If a Christian were struggling with one of the evangelism barriers listed in this chapter, what would you tell them to help them overcome it?

Personal Reflection

1) Does my heart align with God's heart in desiring the lost to be saved? How can I grow in this area?

2) What barriers do I have in my mind that keep me from participating in evangelism? Are any of them addressed in this chapter? How can I get over these barriers?

3) What passage of Scripture is my favorite for reminding me of the importance of evangelism? (Some starting point possibilities if you do not yet have one: Romans 1:14-16; Matthew 5:13-16; Matthew 28:18-20; 2 Corinthians 5:17-21.)

Endnotes for Chapter 2

[1] Barna Group, *Translating the Great Commission: What Spreading the Gospel Means to U.S. Christians in the 21st Century* (Ventura, CA: The Barna Group, 2018), 56f.

[2] David Kinnaman and Gabe Lyons, *Good Faith: Being a Christian When Society Thinks You're Irrelevant and Extreme* (Grand Rapids, MI: Baker Books, 2016), 44f.

[3] Barna Group, *Reviving Evangelism: Current Realities that Demand a New Vision for Sharing Faith* (Ventura, CA: Barna Group, 2019), 10-11.

[4] Barna Group, *Reviving Evangelism,* 10-11.

[5] Barna Group, *Reviving Evangelism,* 5.

[6] Mark Mittelberg, *Building a Contagious Church: Revolutionizing the Way We View and Do Evangelism* (Grand Rapids, MI: Zondervan, 2000), 154.

[7] Kinnaman and Lyons, *Good Faith,* 57.

[8] G.L. Hawkins and Cally Parkinson, *Reveal: Where Are You?* (Barrington, IL: Willow Creek Resources, 2007), 45.

[9] Examples:

Leslie Newbigin, "Evangelism in the Context of Secularization" in *The Study of Evangelism: Exploring a Missional Practice of the Church,* eds. Paul W. Chilcote and Laceye C. Warner (Grand Rapids, MI: Eerdmans, 2008), 48.

George R. Hunsberger, "Is There Biblical Warrant for Evangelism?"

in *The Study of Evangelism: Exploring a Missional Practice of the Church*, eds. Paul W. Chilcote and Laceye C. Warner (Grand Rapids, MI: Eerdmans, 2008), 60-61.

Michael Green, *Evangelism in the Early Church*, Rev. ed. (Grand Rapids, MI: Eerdmans, 2003), 278.

[10] David John Schaal, "Intentional Engagement: Toward an Evangelistic Initiative of Gospel Proclamation," Doctoral diss. (Fuller Theological Seminary, 2020), 92f.

[11] William Rice Broocks Jr., "The Gift of the Evangelist," Doctoral diss. (Fuller Theological Seminary, 2010), 62.

SECTION TWO:
Effective Evangelism in Post-Christian Culture

Chapters 3-12

Chapter 3

Effective Evangelism
in Post-Christian Culture:

God Leads the Way

*"And the hand of the Lord was with them, and a large number
who believed turned to the Lord."*—Acts 11:21

The Best Place to Start

This chapter by itself can change everything—if we are willing to put it into practice. I believe in every principle we will explore about effective evangelism in post-Christian culture; but it is difficult to express how strongly I feel about the one in this chapter.

The main idea is simple, maybe something we already know. However, this is not something to *know*, it is something we must *do*. We see it in Scripture, and I have found it to be true in life and ministry. In fact, I am firmly convinced that if we consistently practice the principle discussed in this chapter, souls will be saved, and the world will be different. And while this principle applies in any context, the challenges of our current culture make it an essential starting point.

It all begins with a powerful theme found in the book of Acts.

God Led the Way

Why did the gospel spread so quickly in the book of Acts? There are several good answers to that question, but they all lead back to one in particular: God led the way.

Jesus promised his disciples that God would be with them in their mission. After instructing them to take the gospel to all nations, the gospel of Matthew ends with Jesus saying, "I am with you always, even to the end of the age." As Acts begins, Jesus tells the apostles they will receive power when the Holy Spirit comes upon them, so they can be his witnesses "in Jerusalem, and in all Judea and Samaria, and even to the remotest part of the earth" (Acts 1:8).

The rest of Acts shows how God kept those promises. He blessed their efforts, in ways bigger than they could have expected. How did he do it? Here are three things to notice:

First, God provided opportunities to share the gospel.

- In Acts 2, God brings the Pentecost crowd together through the sound of a rushing wind and the apostles speaking in other languages. This provided a large audience for Peter's sermon about Jesus.
- In Acts 3, God gives Peter power to heal a lame man, and a Jerusalem crowd gathers again, giving Peter another opportunity to preach.
- In Acts 8:1-4, God uses persecution to bring opportunities for the gospel: the believers are scattered out of Jerusalem, and they start sharing the gospel in other cities.
- In Acts 21, Paul is arrested and will remain in Roman custody for the rest of the book. But God provides opportunities even in those circumstances, as Paul shares the gospel with governors, kings, and others he likely would not have met otherwise.

God provides opportunities for the gospel! Notice that sometimes God acted through miracles, while other times he worked through human choices and natural events. Notice he also worked through hardships; if our eyes are open, even difficult times present opportunities.

Second, God worked in people's lives, preparing them to hear the gospel.

- In Acts 8, the Ethiopian eunuch had worshiped in Jerusalem and was now reading Isaiah on his way home. Through his sincere faith and engagement with Scripture, God had been preparing him to hear the gospel of Jesus.
- In Acts 10, Cornelius was praying, giving generously, and genuinely trying to honor God (Acts 10:1-2). God had already been working in his life and would reward his faith with an opportunity to hear about Jesus.
- God had also been preparing the Jews for generations, with promises about the coming Messiah. In the New Testament, faithful Jews who traveled to Jerusalem for the annual religious feasts had seen Jesus' ministry for several years. They also heard about Jesus' death and resurrection at his final Passover feast. In cities across the Roman Empire, there were Jews looking for the Messiah, allowing Paul to enter synagogues and immediately begin conversations about Jesus (for example: Acts 17:2-3).

Notice that God can prepare people to hear the gospel: through life events and relationships, through their efforts to seek him, through contact with his word.

Third, God brought the timing together.

- In Acts 8, God brings Philip to the Ethiopian's chariot just as he is reading a prophecy about the Messiah and pondering its meaning. A perfect moment for Philip to start talking about Jesus.

- In Acts 16, Paul finds himself in a Philippian prison, with a jailer who needs to hear the gospel. Through a midnight earthquake, the jailer's fear, and Paul's concerned kindness, God arranged the perfect timing for the jailer to ask, "what must I do to be saved?" (v. 30).

- On a bigger scale, the entire gospel story came in God's perfect timing. Jesus came to earth at the right time (Gal. 4:4). Jesus died for us "at the right time" (Rom. 5:6). Scholars have long observed that Christianity entered the world at the perfect moment for its message to spread:[1] the Greek language was spoken everywhere, providing communication across different people groups; the Roman Empire provided relative peace and stability, as well as good transportation; and Jews were living all over the Roman Empire, providing a group in every city that was ready to hear about the Messiah.

God can bring people and events together at the best time for the gospel to be effective. Sometimes God arranges perfect timing for an individual, and sometimes he brings perfect timing to an entire culture.

There is some overlap in the examples above, and several passages could fit multiple categories. Let the main point be clear: God led the way for the gospel in Acts! When Jewish Christians were scattered out of Jerusalem and came to Antioch, Acts 11:21 says, *"the hand of the Lord was with them, and a large number who believed turned to the Lord."* What does it mean that the Lord's hand was with them? God was acting, bringing opportunity and timing together for people he had been preparing to hear.

We see a similar statement when Lydia hears the gospel in Acts 16:14: *"The Lord opened her heart to respond to the things spoken by Paul."* How did God open her heart to hear the gospel? It does not mean God removed her freedom of choice and made her believe. It means the same thing we have seen all over Acts: God had been working in Lydia's life, preparing her to best hear the gospel, and now the opportunity had come in God's perfect timing. She was ready for the message and the gospel took root.

Asking God to Act

Acts highlights the most important reason the gospel spread so rapidly in the first century: God led the way. The natural follow-up question: Can God still guide the spread of the gospel? Absolutely! But we have a role to play in that also: Christians should pray consistently for God to open doors for the gospel. After all, the Bible teaches that sometimes, "you do not have because you do not ask" (James 4:2).

We marvel at how God worked in the early church and in people like the apostle Paul. But one important thing to notice about their efforts to share the gospel: they prayed for God to act. And they prayed a lot. Next time you read Acts, make a note of how often the Christians prayed, including prayers for boldness and for God to lead the way in spreading his word (for example, Acts 4:23-31). Next time you read through Paul's letters, make a note of how often he prays for the churches and reminds Christians to be committed to prayer. Examples include prayers for souls to be saved (Rom. 10:1) and prayers for open doors (Col. 4:2-3). (If you would like to read more about prayer in Acts and Paul's letters, I have put a list of passages in the discussion questions at the end of this chapter.) It is no coincidence that God worked so powerfully through people who prayed so much.

If we believe God's promises about prayer, and if we believe that God has changed the course of history in response to prayer, then we need to be devoted to prayer. Ask for the Lord's hand to bless the spread of the gospel (Acts 11:21). Ask for God to open hearts for the gospel (Acts 16:14). We know God can lead the way, and we know God responds to our prayers. We must put those two truths together and make *evangelistic prayer* a bigger part of our lives.

Becoming People of Evangelistic Prayer

Following the example of Paul and the early church, Christians need to make evangelistic prayer a regular and intentional part of our lives. How do we pray evangelistically? Scripture gives us several good ideas:

1) Pray for the lost.

We all know people who are not right with God, who we hope will change their heart and give their lives to Christ. In Romans 10:1, Paul writes about his fellow Jews who had not yet accepted Jesus:

"Brethren, my heart's desire and my prayer to God for them is for their salvation."

Like Paul, may we feel compassion for lost souls, and may it lead us to pray. Pray that God would soften hearts, stir up spiritual hunger, and bring people into life circumstances that point them back toward him.

Years ago, I came across a simple but powerful two-column worksheet that I still use to this day. In the first column, I wrote the names of five people in my life who were not right with God but who seemed open to a spiritual conversation or invitation. In the second column, I listed five others who did not seem as open. The challenge was to pray for all ten names, every day, and then watch how God would work in their lives.

This practice has been incredibly faith-building. Praying daily for those names, adding names as time goes on, and seeing God's work. It has regularly reminded me that people come to Christ not because of our perfect words or approaches, but because God has been working in their lives, resulting in openness to following Christ. It has also led me to have hard conversations with myself in times when I have let that practice slip. If I genuinely believe God can "open hearts" (Acts 16:14) and "open doors" (Col. 4:3), then I need to be praying persistently. While every person must choose Christ for themselves, God can lead them to moments of clarity, conviction, and openness. He can arrange the right timing and place the right people in their lives. Christians should pray consistently for individuals who are lost, and watch God's work.

2) <u>Pray for those who share the gospel</u>.

In Matthew 9:36-38, Jesus felt compassion for the multitudes, because they were "distressed and dispirited like sheep without a shepherd." That description still fits so many people today. In a broken world full of confusion, pain, and misdirection, countless souls are still searching for the true Shepherd.

What did Jesus tell his disciples to do in response? He said, *"The harvest is plentiful, but the laborers are few; therefore pray earnestly to the Lord of the harvest to send out laborers into His harvest."* (ESV) In other words, pray for more people to stand up and share the good news. That prayer is not just a suggestion—it is a command from Jesus. We should then ask ourselves: Am I praying for more Christians to share their faith? Am I praying for those already sharing the gospel?

In Colossians 4:2-4, Paul asked the Christians to pray for him, a prayer appropriate for all who share the gospel:

> *Devote yourselves to prayer, keeping alert in it with an attitude of thanksgiving; praying at the same time for us as well, that God will open up to us a door for the word so that we may speak forth the mystery of Christ, for which I have also been imprisoned; that I may make it clear in the way I ought to speak.*

Ask God to raise up more Christians who are willing to share their faith. Pray for our preachers and teachers. Pray for missionaries around the world. Pray for all Christians in our conversations and relationships with unbelievers.

The harvest is still plentiful. Christians should pray boldly and regularly for those in the field—and for God to raise up even more.

3) <u>Pray for the church.</u>

Paul's letters are filled with prayers for the churches. One of my personal favorites is Ephesians 3:14-21. Paul prays that God will give the Christians spiritual strength (v. 16). He prays that Christ would live in them and that their lives would be defined by love (v. 17). He prays that they would truly know the love of Christ (v. 19). And then, he reminds us that God can do more through us than we know:

> *Now to Him who is able to do far more abundantly beyond all that we ask or think, according to the power that works within us, to Him be the glory in the church and in Christ Jesus to all generations forever and ever. Amen.* —Ephesians 3:20-21

Like Paul, we need to pray for the church. Pray that Christ would truly live in us and give us strength. Pray that our churches can effectively point people to Christ and help them grow in faith. Pray that God would do more through us than we can even ask or think. When the church is truly bringing glory to God (v. 20), we become a shining light that points people toward him. Like Paul, Christians should pray for Christ's church.

4) <u>Pray for God to work in our culture.</u>

Our culture has been drifting away from Christian principles for decades, and the current conditions tend to discourage people from following Christ.[2] What can we do about that? Give up? Just complain about it? We cannot change the entire culture by ourselves, but we can prayerfully lift up our culture to God, the one who *can* do something about it. In Chapter One, we noted that the same God who has changed the world many times is still working in us today. As history shows, God has arranged events to bring American culture back toward him before; we should pray that he will do so again. Just as missionaries pray for the culture in which they live, we should pray that God would guide our culture to see the goodness of Christianity, allowing faith to flourish and encouraging souls in the right direction instead of the wrong one.

In 1 Chronicles 29:18, David prays for the Israelite nation to have faith, asking God to "direct their heart" toward God. Again, this did not mean that God would control their heart and take away their freedom to choose; David was asking God to work in their lives, putting them in the best possible position to desire God. Christians should pray the same for our own culture.

5) <u>Pray for our own hearts</u>.

We also need to pray for our own hearts to be alive in faith. As David prayed in Psalm 51:10, "*Create in me a clean heart, O God, and renew a steadfast spirit within me.*" Or Psalm 85:6, "*Will You not Yourself revive us again?*" Sometimes a true revival of faith must begin in the lives of God's people; pray that God would help us.

One troubling aspect of post-Christian culture has been the damaging examples set by professing Christians, which have pushed many people away from God.[3] While Christians will never be perfect, we should pray for the authenticity of our own faith—that it would be real and sincere, striving to live for Christ. We will admit our failures along the way and apologize when we fall short, but living for Christ needs to be the honest goal of our life. Many non-Christians desperately need to see a real Christian example in their lives, because they have not seen it before. Christians should pray that God would strengthen our faith, helping us be a positive light to those around us (Matt. 5:14-16).

The Biggest Difference We Can Make

For effective evangelism in our culture, Christians must practice *evangelistic prayer*. Evangelism does not depend on our actions alone;

God's work is far more powerful than anything we can do, and our evangelistic efforts are simply a participation in what God is already doing in people's lives. Bringing souls to God is God's mission, and he leads the way, if only we will show the faith to lean on him. The book of Acts and the letters of Paul show that early Christians prayed constantly for God's strength and help as they shared the gospel in a hostile culture. With such a commitment to prayer, is it any wonder God used them to change the world for him?

If we emphasize evangelistic prayer, this practice alone can make a world-changing difference. Of all the principles in this book, this one may be the easiest to apply, but it could make the biggest impact, because here we are asking God himself to act. As mentioned at the outset of this chapter, the challenge is not merely to *know* the significance of evangelistic prayer, the challenge is to *actually practice* evangelistic prayer. May we commit ourselves to daily prayer for God to lead the way in his evangelism mission, and may we strive to notice the open doors he will put in our path.

Discussion Questions

1) Can you think of someone in the Bible who became a Christian because God brought them to the right place and the right person at the right time in their lives?

2) What does the Bible mean with phrases like "God opened her heart" (Acts16:14)? Does it mean God took away Lydia's freedom of choice? What might God do to help "open hearts" to best hear the gospel?

3) Do you feel like God worked in your life in ways that led to you becoming a Christian? What did God do to help you learn about Christianity and to lead your life to the point where you decided to become a Christian?

4) Take a quick trip through the book of Acts, noticing how much they emphasized prayer. (And notice how the word

"devoted" is often mentioned in connection with their prayer lives.) Some passages to notice: Acts 1:14; 1:24; 2:42; 3:1; 4:23-31; 6:2-7; 10:9; 12:11-12; 13:2-3; 14:23; 16:25. What do you like about those verses? What do we learn from their commitment to prayer? Do you see any connection between their devotion to prayer and God using them to change the world for him?

5) What qualities did Paul have that allowed him to make such a significant impact for Christ? Do not forget that his prayer life was a big part of that! Notice Paul's emphasis on prayer in his writings, in passages such as these: Ephesians 1:15-21; 3:14-21; 6:18-20; Philippians 1:2-4; Colossians 4:2-4.

6) What holds us back from making prayer a bigger part of our lives?

7) Do you believe that God really works in the world in response to the prayers of his people? Can you think of some examples in the Bible of answered prayers? Some passages to remind ourselves of God's promises: Matthew 7:7-11; Luke 11:1-13; James 5:16-18.

8) As we build the habit of evangelistic prayer, what are some specific things for which we can pray?

9) Do you think it is rare for people in our culture to see a "real Christian?" If none of us are perfect, what do we mean by a "real Christian?" Let's pray for our faith to be genuine and to grow!

Personal Reflection

1) Can I name a time in my life when I knew beyond a doubt that God had answered a prayer? How can those experiences give me greater faith in my prayer life?

2) Have I been praying for souls regularly? (Make a list of people in your life as recommended in this chapter and begin praying

daily for God to work in their lives. And then keep your eyes open for opportunities to encourage or invite them!)

3) Would it help if I had another Christian join me in praying regularly for the lost souls in our lives? What fellow Christian or Christians could I ask? This might provide some accountability and encouragement for evangelistic prayer.

4) Do I need a revival of faith in my own life? No one has ever been attracted to the gospel by lukewarm faith. Between me and God, I want to pray that Psalm 51:10 and Psalm 85:6 will become true in my own life.

Endnotes for Chapter 3

[1] Michael Green, *Evangelism in the Early Church*, Rev. ed. (Grand Rapids, MI: Eerdmans, 2003), 29f. This is one example discussing the long-held Christian belief that God prepared the ideal moment for Christianity to spread.

[2] Barna Group, *Reviving Evangelism: Current Realities that Demand a New Vision for Sharing Faith* (Ventura, CA: Barna Group, 2019), 19. This report concluded that "cultural perceptions and Christianity's poor reputation are actively de-converting people raised in church and hardening non-Christians against evangelistic efforts."

[3] *unChristian: What a New Generation Really Thinks About Christianity ... And Why It Matters* (Grand Rapids, MI: Baker Books, 2007), 41-66. Non-Christians believing that they rarely see genuine Christian faith is one of the findings and major theses of the book.

Chapter 4

Effective Evangelism
in Post-Christian Culture:

Patience with a Longer Process

"The Lord is not slow about His promise, as some count slowness, but is patient toward you, not wishing for any to perish but for all to come to repentance." —2 Peter 3:9

Is Everyone Only One Conversation Away?

If you only read certain passages in the New Testament, it might seem that every non-Christian is just one conversation away from becoming a believer. Take Acts 2, for example: Peter preaches a single sermon to the Jewish crowd, and three thousand respond by being baptized (v. 41). In Acts 8, God leads Philip to the Ethiopian eunuch as he returns home. Philip initiates a conversation, they have one Bible study together, and by verse 38 the eunuch is baptized. One time hearing the gospel, and they were ready to commit their lives to Christ.

However, other New Testament passages reveal that the journey to faith is not always so immediate. In Acts 17, Paul preaches at the Areopagus in Athens, and Bible scholars praise the sermon for its brilliance. Paul respectfully builds bridges with the idol-worshiping culture of Athens, acknowledging their religious nature (v. 22), and using their own altar "to an unknown god" (v. 23) as a starting point to introduce the true God.

Quoting their poets, Paul affirms that humanity must seek the living God, and he ultimately brings the message to Jesus and his resurrection. Given the power and relevance of the sermon, we might expect a similar outcome to Peter's, with thousands responding in faith.

But that is not what happens. Acts 17:34 records a modest response: "Some men joined him and believed, among whom also were Dionysius the Areopagite and a woman named Damaris and others with them." Instead of thousands, we find a modest response, small enough to mention a few individual names. Earlier in verse 32, we are told that some sneered and others were merely curious, saying they wanted to hear more. Most of Paul's audience was not ready to believe after just one message. For them, the path to faith would take more time.

We also see a longer process to faith in 1 Peter 3:1-2, where Peter counsels Christian wives who had unbelieving husbands:

In the same way, you wives, be submissive to your own husbands so that even if any of them are disobedient to the word, they may be won without a word by the behavior of their wives, as they observe your chaste and respectful behavior.

Notice he speaks of husbands who had already heard the gospel message, because they had been "disobedient" to it. Their issue was not lack of information, so Peter does not encourage more teaching; rather, he urges the wives to speak "without a word" through their consistent Christian character. Through quiet example and steady love, the hope was that over time, these husbands might become more open to faith. They were not one conversation away from becoming Christians; their hearts needed to be softened by example and time.

Why the Difference?

Why were some people in the New Testament ready to become Christians after one sermon or conversation, while others needed a longer process? One factor that led to the quick responses: God had orchestrated a perfect moment for the gospel to spread among the Jews. There were Jews throughout the Roman Empire who had been following God their entire life. They knew the Scriptures, they were looking for the Messiah, and Old Testament prophecies such as Daniel 2:44-45 had led them to believe that the Messiah and his kingdom should be arriving at any time. Many of those faithful Jews simply needed to be told about the life of Jesus, and how he fulfilled those Messianic prophecies they had known their entire life.

That is why the Jews in Acts 2 were ready to be baptized so quickly—after all, they had traveled to Jerusalem for the Pentecost feast, showing their hearts were already committed to God, they just had not connected the Scriptures to Jesus yet. The same was true for the Ethiopian eunuch in Acts 8. He had come to Jerusalem to worship and was reading from Isaiah as Philip approached. He was already devoted to God; he simply needed someone to tell him that Jesus was the fulfillment of what he was reading. This is also why, as Paul traveled from town to town, he always began in the Jewish synagogues (Acts 17:1–2). He knew that many of the Jews were only one conversation away from recognizing Jesus as the Messiah and giving their lives to him.

But of course, others began further away from Christianity. The people of Athens in Acts 17 had far less exposure to God's truth. They worshiped idols and had no understanding of the one true God, so that's where Paul began his sermon. They did not know or believe in the Jewish Scriptures, so Paul did not quote from them. They had not seen Jesus teach, heal, or perform miracles at the Jerusalem feasts, like faithful Jews had seen for years. They would need a longer process of learning about God, Scripture, Jesus, and Christianity, before they could make the life decision to follow Christ.

In some cases, knowledge was not the problem. Some simply were not receptive to the gospel, even among the Jews. Many of the Jewish leaders knew all about Jesus' life and the Old Testament prophecies, but they did not want to hear that the one they sent to the cross was the Messiah. In Acts chapters 3-7, we see their resistance intensify until a full-scale persecution begins in Acts 8:1-4. Saul, who was not yet a Christian and who later became known as Paul, played a significant role in that persecution. As he would later describe it, he was "a persecutor and violent aggressor" against Christianity (1 Tim. 1:13). But Saul did not merely lack knowledge about Jesus; he lacked a receptive heart. His hostility grew and his heart was resistant until God intervened (Acts 9:1-22) and changed the course of his life. (Remember our prayer discussion from the last chapter, God can do that!)

The passages above show that two key factors influenced how quickly an individual could embrace the gospel: *knowledge* and *receptivity*.[1] Some people had prior knowledge of God and Jesus, while others required more learning before they could accept the gospel. And some were eagerly receptive to the gospel of Christ, while others were simply not open to receiving the message. Both factors are still relevant today.

What About Our Culture?

In our culture, are most unbelievers just one conversation away from becoming Christians or do they usually require a longer journey? While it certainly varies from person to person, the reality is that most non-Christians in our context will need a longer process before they are ready to commit to Christ. Both knowledge and receptivity may require more time. On the knowledge side, as we saw in Chapter One, many people in post-Christian culture think they already know the Christian message, even though many have only heard it through media stereotypes and caricatures.[2] Unbelievers in our culture usually begin with less biblical understanding and very different ideas about truth,[3] so a Christian worldview will initially seem foreign and must be developed. It will take time for the average unbelieving American to process the truths of Christianity; their knowledge about true Christianity is starting from much farther away.

Receptivity can be just as problematic. Studies show that people in modern American culture are generally less open to Christianity and feel less of a spiritual need than previous generations.[4] The secular push against Christianity has convinced many that our faith should be rejected without giving it a fair hearing, making them less open to exploring Christian truths. The finding that our culture is less inclined to feel spiritual needs is both interesting and disappointing. Perhaps our endless media and entertainment distractions prevent us from slowing down and reflecting on spiritual matters? Whatever the causes, the result is that fewer individuals are searching for God and truth compared to previous generations.

Thom Rainer's research charted the receptivity factor in American culture, grouping unbelievers according to their openness to the gospel. He identified five levels of receptivity:[5]

> U5 – Highly resistant to the gospel, antagonistic attitude
>
> U4 – Resistant to the gospel, but not an antagonistic attitude
>
> U3– No apparent receptivity, neutral, perhaps open to discussion
>
> U2 – Receptive to the gospel and to the church
>
> U1 – Highly receptive to the gospel, "the Philippian jailer"

Rainer's goal in defining these categories was to help Christians recognize that people are starting at different levels of receptivity. The more resistant they are to the gospel, the more likely it will take a longer process to come to Christ.

Research supports the idea that conversions in our context typically involve a longer process. For one example, a recent study of new converts in the northeastern states found that 86% came to faith through multiple conversations over months or years, as opposed to a single conversation or a short period of time.[6] Since people in our culture often start further away in both knowledge and receptivity, they will require a longer path of thinking and processing before they decide to follow Christ.

Patience in Sharing Our Faith

The implications are clear: as we share our faith, we must learn to be patient, recognizing that the process of committing to Christ in our culture will often take time. While waiting is not always easy, patience is an evangelistic trait of God himself, and one we must seek to emulate. As Paul reflected on his life change from persecutor to committed Christian, he wrote that Jesus Christ showed "His perfect patience as an example for those who would believe in Him" (1 Tim. 1:16). God's patience in Paul's life transformation is an example to sinners that God can indeed turn their life around, and it also serves as an example to Christians: God patiently waited for Paul to commit to Christ, and we must show similar patience.

2 Peter 3:9 says that God even delays the coming of Christ because he is being patient with souls: *"The Lord is not slow about His promise, as some count slowness, but is patient toward you, not wishing for any to perish but for all to come to repentance."* God knows when people will turn to him and when they will not, and he is guiding the world's timeline accordingly. Not only do we see God's patience with people in Scripture, but we as Christians today can also express gratitude for his patience in our own lives. We have all sinned and taken wrong spiritual turns, and yet God patiently allowed us time to learn, grow, and come back to him.

Why is it difficult to be patient with a longer process of people coming to Christ? Sometimes it is our own busyness or unwillingness to walk alongside people for months or years before they are ready to make the Christian commitment. But for many Christians, the greater challenge is feeling the urgency of the gospel, leading us to encourage people towards quicker decisions. We realize that one's soul is most important, that life is a vapor, and that tomorrow is not promised (Jas. 4:14). We know eternity is real, and we do not want anyone to face it without Christ. That sense of urgency is good, and we should not eliminate those biblical truths from our mindset. However, we must balance biblical urgency with the biblical truth that God is patient and that he is guiding lives and even the world's timeline to allow souls to come to him.

We must also remember that if we push too quickly, we do not allow genuine, soul-saving faith to grow. Jesus and Paul compared the gospel message to a seed (Luke 8:11, 1 Cor. 3:6-8), and seeds require time to grow. You cannot force the seeds in your garden to grow more quickly. Over-watering does not speed up the process, and it could even kill the plant!

The same is true for growth in our children; we realize that growth takes time. You cannot push a newborn baby to run, or talk, or eat solid food. They are not ready, and pushing those things too quickly is more likely to hurt than help. They must be taught and encouraged at the right pace. I cannot push my fifth-grade daughter to learn calculus; she is many steps away from calculus, and forcing that too quickly will only frustrate both of us. Learning math and other school subjects must come at the right pace. The same is true of spiritual growth: the seeds of the gospel take time to grow in all of us, and we want to nurture the process in others. But we cannot push the process too quickly or real growth will not happen.

Patiently Encouraging the Next Step

We must develop wisdom as we interact with those who are not yet Christians. We want to encourage people toward Christ without pushing them inappropriately. It is possible to push people toward a faith decision too quickly and inappropriately, which often results in people feeling pressured or manipulated, and many react by pulling away from Christianity.

In fact, this is one of our culture's common criticisms about Christians: that too many believers are relationally inappropriate in the way they share the gospel.[7] It is true that some people may use this as an excuse to avoid the claims of Christianity. But in many cases, the critique reveals something important: non-Christians might actually be open to talking about our faith, if only we would approach the subject differently,[8] with less pressure and anxiety.

While it is possible to push too quickly, we must also be careful not to swing too far in the other direction and avoid the subject entirely. In our desire not to offend, we may end up staying silent when God wants us to speak. We must pray that God would bless us with wisdom as we seek the appropriate levels of patience and encouragement with those who are not yet Christians (Jas. 1:5; Col. 4:5-6).

How can we develop the wisdom to encourage non-Christians toward Christ without pushing too quickly? In addition to prayer, one way is to ask ourselves: *what is the next step that will bring this person closer to Christ?* It may help to visualize the process as a series of steps. Or as I heard it explained in a class once, as a series of dominos that need to be knocked down over time.[9]

For example, imagine a non-Christian adult in America. In this imagined scenario, we meet a man who rarely went to a church growing up, so he has little knowledge about the Bible and no strong Christians among his family or close friends. From all he has heard in the media, he has become very resistant to Christianity, deciding somewhere along the way that Christians are fake, hypocritical, and maybe a little crazy. Ask yourself: what is it going to take for someone like him to become a Christian? It is not going to be one conversation or sermon, is it? Here are some possible "dominos" that might need to fall for him to eventually become a Christian:

- He might have to meet someone who is a genuine Christian and realize that they are a "real person."

- He might need to have several faith conversations with that person or another Christian and see that Christianity is a strength to people and blesses their lives.
- He might need to be invited to a church service or event, and he might need invitations to happen several times at appropriate intervals before he agrees to come to one.
- He might need something difficult to happen in his life to help him start thinking about deeper spiritual matters.
- He might need to hear a Christian say that they are praying for him.
- He might need to see Christians doing good things for others, showing him that their faith is unselfish and real.
- He might need to notice from experience or observation that a sinful life leads to pain and that what the sinful world offers is always empty at the end.
- He might need to be greeted kindly by Christians when he finally visits a worship service.
- He might need to hear a certain song or sermon that helps him reflect on the goodness and truth of Christianity.
- He might need to see that Christians really love each other and try to help each other through life.
- He might need conversations or studies with a Christian about nagging questions he still has about Christianity.
- He might need to really believe that Christians will be patient with him and support him if he truly makes the commitment to live for Christ.
- He might need to get over the fear of his friends or family finding out he wants to be baptized into Christ.

Perhaps you could add other dominos to that list, but may we see the point: those things will not all happen in one conversation, or one week, or maybe not in a year or more. But here is the good news that Christians can affirm: these types of life stories do happen! God works in people's lives over time—especially as we keep praying for them—and most of our churches have people who could tell their story of coming to Christ over years or decades.

So, a great way to think evangelistically is to ask ourselves: what is the next domino that needs to fall in this person's path to becoming a Christian? We may not be able to help them knock all the dominos down, but we can try to encourage the next one, and trust God and his people to keep working in their life even if we are not around to see the entire process come together.

Seeing It in My Own Life

"Evangelistic patience" is a principle I wish I had known years ago. One example of many came when I was 21 years old. I was working at an express oil change shop in my hometown for about eight months, saving up money so I could transfer to a new university to study Bible and ministry. To put it mildly, my coworkers at the oil change shop were not Christians. But as we got to know each other, they learned what I was doing there and what I planned to do in life, which led to some good conversations, and we all became friends by the time I left. (In fact, that is one of my life experiences that convinced me non-Christians in our culture are indeed interested in and willing to discuss Christianity, if only we will discuss it the right way. We will say even more about that issue in Chapters 8 and 9.)

Our manager's name was Jon. Jon was a generation older than most of us, and while Jon was not a Christian and did not pretend to be, he showed a kindness toward me and an interest in my life goals that I appreciated. Before my eight months ended, I finally decided that I needed to ask Jon to sit down and have a real Bible study together. He agreed, and I was excited as I drove up to his house, my Bible in hand. Over the next hour or two—poor Jon—I think I shared everything I knew about Christianity: why we believe in God; why we believe the Bible is from God; why we believe in Jesus and how to become a Christian; what the Bible says about the church and following the teachings of the apostles. Jon listened kindly, even asking some good questions and contributing some good thoughts, but by the end of our time together his eyes were predictably glazed over.

I was trying to accomplish *way* too much in my study with Jon. In the language of this chapter, I was trying to knock over all the dominos that stood between Jon becoming a committed Christian, all by myself, and all in one conversation. I wish I had understood the principle of patience and looking for the next domino. A few dominos had already come down in Jon's life through our conversations that summer. I wish I had learned the wisdom to patiently pursue the next ones. Maybe starting a weekly Bible study to slowly discuss a variety of topics, instead of one long marathon conversation. Maybe an invitation to visit our church with me. Maybe getting coffee to introduce Jon to our preacher, who I think he would have enjoyed meeting and could have continued the conversations long after I left to begin my new program.

I trust God has continued to work in Jon's life long after our time of knowing each other, and I know he must make his own faith decisions between himself and God. But looking back at that experience, I recognize the importance of evangelistic patience. Non-Christians in our culture will often need more time before they are ready to give their lives to Christ. They may need to grow in both knowledge and receptivity to the gospel. It probably will not happen in one conversation, so we do not need to push people too far, too fast. But we *do* need to be asking, "what is the next step for this person to come closer to Christ?", and we need to try to encourage that next step in any way we can. Patience does not mean inaction; it means we continue to pray and keep our eyes open for opportunities to help with the next domino. Over time, God works in people's lives, providing the increase for the gospel's seeds to grow, and we may get to see the moment when people are finally ready to make the biggest, best decision of their lives.

Making It Part of Our Faith-Sharing Perspective

For effective evangelism in our culture, Christians must practice *evangelistic patience.* This is an important mindset shift for post-Christian evangelism! When we recognize that a non-Christian coming to Christ will likely be a longer process, we can be more patient and engage in more effective, appropriate ways. We can be less pushy for quick decisions. We can think in terms of multiple conversations rather than feeling pressure to download too much information in a single conversation. We can allow non-Christians the time to ask questions and express doubts, and there is no need for us to feel threatened or respond anxiously as we discuss those issues with them. We can recognize that God will keep working in the non-Christian's life even after we have a single, likely-imperfect faith conversation. We can remember that we are not the only person God can use to help the process along. We can realize that helping people simply move one step closer to faith, in knowledge or receptivity or both, may be seen as a success toward the bigger goal.[10] Remember also that people must make their own decisions between themselves and God, so our job is not to push or manipulate; we are simply trying to be encouragers for the gospel. Pray that God will give us patience and wisdom as we encourage souls closer to him.

Discussion Questions

1) Was everyone in the New Testament just one conversation away from becoming a Christian? Why were some people closer to becoming Christians than others?

2) What characteristics of our culture suggest that it will often take a longer process for people to come to Christ? Do you agree that people in our culture may start further away from Christianity than previous generations in both knowledge and receptivity?

3) What passages of Scripture remind us that God is patient with people who are not yet Christians?

4) What are some reasons it may be difficult for Christians to be patient with a longer process of people coming to Christ?

5) If we are committed to convincing everyone to become a Christian in a single conversation, how might that lead us to speak or act in ways that hurt the possibility they will give their lives to Christ?

6) Do you like to be pressured or pushed into major life decisions? Why or why not? How might that affect the way we speak to people about their faith?

7) Who was patient with you as you came to Christ? Or as you grew in your faith? What impact might it have had if someone had been impatient with you?

8) Brainstorm some of the "dominos" that may need to fall for an average unchurched American adult to eventually become a committed Christian. How long might it take for those things to happen?

9) How can we balance the urgency of the gospel with the patience of the gospel? Is it possible to be "too patient?" Is there a right time to emphasize urgency, and how can we know when that time is? Will we always get the balance right between urgency and patience?

10) Are there any advantages to someone slowly deciding to become a Christian, as opposed to making a quick decision after one sermon or conversation?

Personal Reflection

1) Are there times in my life when I wish I had known the "patience principle" in sharing the gospel? What might I have done differently? (Note: This is not to beat yourself up—God will continue working in that person's life, and they must take

responsibility for their own soul decisions. The goal is simply to reflect and learn, and then do our best with the next opportunity God gives us.)

2) Who in my life is ready for the "next domino?" What is it, and what can I do to encourage it?

Endnotes for Chapter 4

[1] Some authors and scholars have attempted to chart these two factors (knowledge and receptivity), helping Christians visualize the process by which people come to faith. The "Engel Evangelism Scale" attempted to chart different pieces of knowledge that contributed to people becoming Christians (James Engel and Hugo Wilbert Norton, *What's Gone Wrong with the Harvest? A Communication Strategy for the Church and World Evangelization* (Grand Rapids: Zondervan, 1975)). Later, Thom Rainer's research studies attempted to chart the receptivity factor in American culture, identifying five levels of openness to the gospel, ranging from highly resistant to highly receptive (Rainer, *The Unchurched Next Door: Understanding Faith Stages as Keys to Sharing Your Faith (Grand Rapids, MI: Zondervan, 2003)*, summary chart, p. 21). Others, such as the Gray Matrix, attempt to chart both knowledge and receptivity on the same x-y graph (The Gray Matrix, https://thegraymatrix.org/index.php/the-matrix/).

[2] David M. Gustafson, *Gospel Witness: Evangelism in Word and Deed* (Grand Rapids, MI: Eerdmans, 2019) 5.

[3] Will McRaney, Jr., *The Art of Personal Evangelism: Sharing Jesus in a Challenging Culture* (Nashville, TN: Broadman and Holman, 2003), 3-4.

[4] These all seen in McRaney's list, *The Art of Personal Evangelism*, 3-4. The low sense of spiritual need is also seen in: Barna Group: *Reviving Evangelism: Current Realities that Demand a New Vision for Sharing Faith*(Ventura, CA: Barna Group, 2019), 12,19

[5] Rainer, *The Unchurched Next Door*, summary chart, 21.

[6] Gary S. Comer, *Soul Whisperer: Why the Church Must Change the Way It Views Evangelism* (Eugene, OR: Resource Publications, 2013), 142.

[7] Examples of evangelism approaches that were received as socially inappropriate or unkind:

David Kinnaman and Gabe Lyons, *unChristian: What a New Generation Really Think About Christianity ... And Why It Matters* (Grand Rapids, MI: Baker Books, 2007), 67-90.

John P. Bowen, *Evangelism for "Normal" People: Good News for Those Looking for a Fresh Approach* (Minneapolis, MN: Augsburg Fortress, 2002), 19, 23.

[8] Bowen, *Evangelism for "Normal" People*, 23. This was his conclusion after relating several stories of inappropriate evangelism approaches and how non-Christians described them later.

[9] I first heard this concept shared by Dr. Steve Cloer in a class titled *Evangelism, Discipleship, and Church Planting* at Harding School of Theology, Memphis, TN, Summer semester 2022.

[10] McRaney, *The Art of Personal Evangelism*, 50.

Chapter 5

Effective Evangelism
in Post-Christian Culture:

Finding My Place in the Mission

"Since we have gifts that differ according to the grace given to us, each of us is to exercise them accordingly." —Romans 12:6

Maybe I Am Just Not an Evangelist?

When you picture someone who is good at evangelism, what comes to mind? Probably someone outgoing, quick with the right answers, naturally charismatic, and who can instantly connect on a deep level with complete strangers. It is easy to assume that effective evangelism requires a specific kind of personality. And when we do not see those traits in ourselves, many Christians conclude, "Maybe I am just not built to be good at evangelism."

When I was growing up, there was a Christian man in my hometown named Willie. When I thought about a prototypical evangelist, I always thought of him. A former NFL football player, he had a big personality that naturally drew a crowd. Willie loved people and people loved Willie. Everywhere he went, he had conversations with people about their faith. He naturally projected a sense of bold spiritual strength, and his personality made others want to be stronger themselves. He had the ability to tell someone he just met that they needed to get their life right and start coming to church with him, and most of the time they would agree with him. It was incredible to watch.

While I marveled at Willie's ability to inspire faith in others, another thought subconsciously lingered in the back of my mind: I could never really do that. I mean, how many people are like that? That is just not most people's personality. If that is what a good evangelist looks like—and Willie was undeniably good at it—I guess I simply could not be a good evangelist. I think many Christians wrestle with those same feelings. They see people with big personalities who are effective at evangelism, and they shrug to themselves, quietly listing the reasons they do not think their personality is built for evangelism:

- I am not outgoing enough.
- I never know what to say when people start talking about religion.
- People do not seem to listen to me like they do other people.

Do we just have to depend on the outgoing, have-all-the-answers Christians to handle evangelism, while the rest of us sit on the sideline wishing we could help?

Evangelism "Personalities"?

In the many evangelism writings of the past few decades, one of the favorite themes to emerge is the concept of evangelism personalities.[1] It is both biblical and helpful, and it has been described by one writer as "a significant contribution to the field of evangelism."[2] Another says he has "never found a concept that better liberates people who have written off evangelism as something that's not for them."[3] So if you are tempted to think that evangelism is only for extroverts or people of superhuman religious knowledge, I believe you will truly appreciate this concept. As still another writer praises it: "the genius of this approach is that it recognizes that there are many different biblical models of doing outreach,"[4] allowing

Christians to see that Scripture itself shows different personalities engaging in evangelism in diverse ways.

That makes sense, because the Bible describes the church as a body made up of many different members, with each member contributing unique talents and abilities. Each person's talents are needed, blending together to serve God. Notice what Paul says in Romans 12:4-6:

> *For just as we have many members in one body and all the members do not have the same function, so we, who are many, are one body in Christ, and individually members one of another. Since we have gifts that differ according to the grace given to us, each of us is to exercise them accordingly. ...*

We find the same teaching in 1 Corinthians 12:12-27, another passage in which the church is described as a body with many different members. As Paul explains the analogy, just because the foot is not a hand does not mean that the foot is not part of the body; both the foot and the hand have distinct roles, and both are needed for the body to function well. The same is true for eyes and ears. Just because your talents are different from another Christian's does not mean you have no role to play. Your role will be different but just as important.

We already understand this principle in many areas of church life, such as our times of worship. Everyone worships together, but we ask those with specific abilities to help lead us. We ask those who can lead singing to do so. We ask those who can prepare and present God's word to teach or preach. I may not be the song leader or the prayer leader or the preacher, but I am still expected to participate fully, contributing my presence, my singing voice, and my heart in worship. Distinct roles, all important, brought together to do what the church is meant to do.

Evangelism works the same way. In Ephesians 4:11-16, Paul applies the church-body analogy to God's plan for building up his church. Paul says that God planned for some people—not everyone—to serve in certain teaching roles, such as evangelists and teachers (Eph. 4:11). And those who serve in such roles are supposed to "equip the saints for the work of service, to the building up of the body of Christ" (Eph. 4:12). Those verses remind us that not every Christian serves in the role of an evangelist or a teacher, as James 3:1 also says ("Let not many of you become teachers"). While we all hope to mature in our faith and be able to share Christian truth with others (1 Pet. 3:15, Heb. 5:12), the Bible acknowledges that not every Christian will be a teacher. But Ephesians 4:11-12 also tells us that every Christian *should* be equipped to serve God in ways that build up the body of Christ, whether that is a teaching role or not. Ephesians 4:16 then describes what happens when we are all serving in our different ways: when we are "fitted and held together by what every joint supplies, according to the proper working of each individual part," Jesus Christ uses our different efforts and "causes the growth of the body for the building up of itself in love."

Evangelism is meant to be a team effort of God's church. Remember what we studied in Chapter Two: Matthew 28:18-20 is not a command for a single individual, it is a group command for the entire church:

And Jesus came up and spoke to them, saying, "All authority has been given to Me in heaven and on earth. Go therefore and make disciples of all the nations, baptizing them in the name of the Father and the Son and the Holy Spirit, teaching them to observe all that I commanded you; and lo, I am with you always, even to the end of the age."

No single person can fulfill that command alone because no one person can make disciples of every single nation on earth all by themselves. The evangelistic task is given to all Christians, lasting until "the end of the age." This is not a command only for you as an individual. This is a command from Jesus to His church as a corporate body. And like any command from

Jesus to his church, we all contribute our different talents to serve him together.

Every Christian should be part of God's evangelistic mission, whether we consider ourselves to be "gifted" for evangelism or not. The basic principle of "evangelism personalities" is that we each contribute to that mission in different ways. As one writer summarizes the idea: "If each person does what they are gifted to do, however insignificant any individual piece may seem, a rich tapestry of evangelism will result."[5]

Explaining the Evangelism Personalities

What are the different evangelism personalities? The lists vary in different sources,[6] but they all attempt to look at the New Testament and see how Christians contributed to God's evangelistic mission in various ways. Here is a slightly modified version of the first list I saw on this concept:[7]

1) The Direct Style of Peter in Acts 2.
2) The Intellectual Style of Paul in Acts 17.
3) The Share-My-Story Style of the Blind Man in John 9.
4) The Relationship-Building Style of Matthew in Luke 5.
5) The Invitational Style of the Samaritan Woman in John 4.
6) The Serving Style of Dorcas in Acts 9.

Following the usual approach of evangelism personality studies, we will explore what is meant by each of the personalities on that list and how they contribute to the church's evangelistic mission.

1)   The Direct Style of Peter in Acts 2 –

In Acts 2, the Holy Spirit comes upon the twelve apostles and a crowd gathers in response. All twelve apostles begin talking in different languages, but it is Peter who speaks up and delivers the sermon. That does not surprise us—Peter had always been bold, quick to speak, and unafraid to act.

When the opportunity came to share the truth about Jesus—his life, death, resurrection, and ascension, and how the crowd was guilty before God—Peter was the perfect person for the task. In fact, Peter's boldness continues throughout the book of Acts (read Acts chapters 3–5 and notice Peter's bold, outspoken faith), and at every step, it resulted in more people becoming Christians.

While our post-Christian culture tends to dislike confrontation or anything that feels like pressure, there is still an important place for bold, direct evangelism. Some people—like Willie, whom I mentioned at the start of this chapter—have a natural gift for direct, real conversations with others, in ways that people recognize as authentic and coming from genuine faith and love. People usually respond well to the authenticity of Christians with this evangelism personality; and even when their direct approach is initially rejected, it is often remembered later with respect.

We all know people who made a lasting impact on our lives because they spoke plainly and truthfully. Sometimes that is just what we need to hear. Keep your eyes open for moments when a direct word about faith is necessary, and pray for God to give wisdom and courage when those moments arise. For some Christians, this is your natural personality, and the church needs you to be you! Look for opportunities to have direct conversations with people and encourage them to follow Jesus.

2) The Intellectual Style of Paul in Acts 17 –

In Acts 17, Paul's second missionary journey brings him to the proud intellectual city of Athens. The first thing Paul does—and we love this about Paul—is to go out and start talking with people in the city. He goes to the synagogue on Sabbath days to talk with the Jews gathering for worship, and he goes into the marketplace every day, to talk with "those who happened to be present" (Acts 17:16-17). Those conversations lead to an opportunity for Paul to preach at the Athens Areopagus, where he addresses a crowd full of idol-worshipers. As we noticed in Chapter Four, the Athenians did not know much about the true God, so Paul starts his sermon further back, explaining God as the creator and then leading to Jesus and the resurrection. A few people became Christians at the end of the sermon, while others wanted to hear more.

Paul's life experiences made him the perfect person for this type of evangelism. Remember, Paul had the best education of any apostle, studying in Jerusalem under the rabbi Gamaliel (Acts 22:3). He could discuss Old Testament passages with the Jews or quote Greek poets with the Gentiles. He had lived both in Jewish Jerusalem and Gentile Tarsus. His education and experiences made him the perfect person to go out and start talking with people, discussing ideas and showing people the truth of Christianity, whether in synagogues, marketplaces, or the Athens Areopagus.

Our post-Christian culture tends to be skeptical about truth claims, including the truths taught in Christianity, so we need Christians who are interested in digging into ideas and discussing why we believe Christianity is true and right. In the time I have been in ministry, I can already see how the questions change from generation to generation, reminding me that each generation and culture will have different questions. We want to help provide answers to those who are genuinely asking, so they can overcome whatever barriers are holding them back from following Christ. Among churches of Christ, Apologetics Press is one organization that focuses on this area of evangelism, providing a valuable resource for the rest of us to have these conversations. If you have a personality that enjoys these issues and discussions, the church needs you to be you! Look to engage our culture's questions, and in a spirit of genuine Christian love, discuss these issues with others and show the world the truth of the Christian faith.

3) The Share-My-Story Style of the Blind Man in John 9 –

In John 9, Jesus gives sight to a blind man. The Jews bring the man to the Pharisees, who were already jealous of Jesus, and they immediately decide that Jesus cannot be from God because he healed the man on a Sabbath day (vv. 13-16). As the entire event becomes a debate about Jesus' identity, the Pharisees again turn to the man who was given sight, hoping he will stop giving credit to Jesus, whom they call a sinner: "Give glory to God, we know that this man is a sinner" (v. 24). We love the man's answer in verse 25:

He then answered, "Whether He is a sinner I do not know; one thing I do know, that though I was blind, now I see."

What a great response! He does not claim to have all the answers, and he does not get into debates about healing on the Sabbath or how Jesus got his power. He simply tells what he knows, because it happened to him: I could not see, Jesus gave me sight, and now I see.

In our post-Christian culture, people do not always want to hear a sermon or a direct confrontation about how they should change their lives for Christ. However, most people will listen respectfully to someone's personal experiences about their faith. What a great open door in our culture! You do not have to know the answers to every question or be an expert in theology, you simply need to be able to tell others the difference that faith has made in your life.

For some Christians, this fits their personality, so in conversations with friends and non-Christians, they are able to share naturally how faith has impacted them: how Christ gave them strength through times of difficulty; how their church family rallied around them during a health scare; how they were struggling with sin but God helped them get away from it; how faith and hope gives them peace when the world seems to be going crazy. Those conversations plant seeds of faith, letting unbelievers see that Christianity really makes a difference in life. May we all be looking for opportunities to plant those seeds, and if "sharing your story" fits your natural personality, the church needs you to be you! It is certainly biblical: as Jesus told another man he healed, "Go home to your people and report to them what great things the Lord has done for you" (Mark 5:19). Be looking for opportunities to share the good things you have seen in your faith.

4) <u>The Relationship-Building Style of Matthew in Luke 5</u> –

In Luke 5:27, Jesus calls Levi (also known as Matthew) to leave his career as a tax collector and follow him. One of the great examples in the Bible, Levi "left everything behind, and got up and began to follow Him" (v. 28). And then notice what Levi did in verse 29:

And Levi gave a big reception for Him in his house; and there was a great crowd of tax collectors and other people who were reclining at the table with them.

What a great idea! Levi gave a "reception" for Jesus. The tax collectors were probably friends of Levi, people he had known and invited, wanting them to meet Jesus. As the following verses show, Jesus and the disciples were there, along with those tax collectors and people whom the Pharisees called sinners (v. 30). When the Pharisees complained that Jesus would spend time with such people, Jesus responded that he came to call sinners to repentance (vv. 31-32). Sinners needed to meet Jesus and his followers, giving them opportunities to grow closer to God through those relationships.

As our post-Christian culture gets more technology-focused and more relationally isolated,[8] genuine relationship-building stands out more and more. And that is important, because most conversions to Christianity come through a personal relationship. (We will study that principle more in Chapter Seven.) God made us social beings, and people appreciate when they are shown kindness and genuine relationship.

Some people excel at building relationships. Perhaps your personality naturally connects with others, making it easy for you to become part of people's lives. You meet someone along life's path, and soon you are talking about life issues, getting coffee together, or having them over for dinner. Relationships are an important pathway to help people see genuine Christian examples, so we need more relationship-builders. If this is your natural personality, the church needs you to be you! Look for opportunities to build genuine relationships with those whom God puts in your path, and they will see faith living in you.

5) <u>The Invitational Style of the Samaritan Woman in John 4</u> –

In John 4, Jesus meets a Samaritan woman at the well, and in one conversation, she realizes that he is at least a prophet, and maybe even the long-awaited Messiah. She rushes back to the city and gives a simple invitation in verse 29: *"Come, see a man who told me all the things that I have done; this is not the Christ, is it?"* You might notice some "Share-My-Story" style in that also, but she turned her story into an invitation. We also notice that she is not debating religious ideas or preaching at people; she is simply telling that she has seen something special and inviting others to come see for themselves. In verse 30, the people come out of the city to meet Jesus, and many believe in him (v. 41). The woman's invitation brought them to Jesus, and it led them to develop their own faith in him.

In fact, invitations are all over the early chapters of John's gospel. In John 1:40-42, Andrew invites his brother Simon (who will soon be known as Peter) to come meet Jesus, an invitation that will change Simon's life and impact the history of the world. In John 1:43-49, Philip invites Nathanael to come meet Jesus, and it is not long before Nathanael also becomes a follower of Jesus. Notice again in these examples: there was no religious debating, no pressure. It was simply an invitation. In these cases, the invitations were accepted, and soon those who were invited began growing in their own faith.

In our post-Christian culture, you might be surprised to know that most non-Christians say they would attend a church worship service or event if a Christian friend or family member invited them. (We will explore this idea more in Chapter Ten). What a great open door for the gospel! Some people are good at this. It is natural for them to invite someone to come to worship or a church get-together, just as they would invite someone to a ballgame or lunch or anything else they enjoy in life. When you can combine "Relationship-Building" with "Invitational" styles, it is even more effective, giving people an opportunity to meet their church family and think about their own relationship with God. We all need to be looking for inviting opportunities, but if this is your natural personality, the church needs you to be you! Look for opportunities to invite people and watch how God can work in those situations.

6) The Serving Style of Dorcas in Acts 9 –

In Acts 9, a Christian woman named Tabitha (also called Dorcas) passed away. God would show his power by using Peter to raise her back to life. As we read about this amazing event, we learn something special about Dorcas: she was a woman who loved to serve others. Look at the description the Bible gives her in Acts 9:36: *"this woman was abounding with deeds of kindness and charity which she continually did."* (What a great way for the Bible to describe you!) As the widows were bringing Peter to Dorcas' room, they were "showing him all the tunics and garments that Dorcas used to make" (v. 39). Dorcas was talented, and she used her talents to serve others.

In a post-Christian culture that often claims Christians are just a bunch of hypocrites,[9] serving others is an important way to show the genuine goodness of the Christian faith, which opens doors for the gospel. Several years ago, our church was one of many that sent a group to the Gulf Coast to help a small town recover from a recent hurricane. As the team tore out water-soaked walls and cleaned up trash-covered yards, one thankful resident asked them a simple but powerful question: "Why are you all doing this?" One of our young adults was able to share that the entire trip was based in our Christian faith, desiring to show God's love to others. I hope it planted a seed of faith that would grow long after the group came back home. One writer suggests that the biggest religious skeptics often become more receptive by seeing genuine Christian acts of service.[10]

May we strive to serve others, just as Christ served us (John 13:12-17; 34-35). And if your personality leans toward showing love and acts of service, the church needs you to be you! Look for opportunities to show God's love, and watch God work through your Christlike example.

Sharing the Gospel, Together

For effective evangelism in our culture, we need every Christian contributing to the mission in their own *evangelism personalities*. Evangelism is never just a one-person-show; it is a collective mission that stretches far beyond any individual. God works in people's lives, long before we ever meet them. And then, when the church functions as it should, each member contributes toward the larger goal, and together we encourage souls toward Christ.

As I think back over the people who have come to Christ during my time in ministry, I realize their journey often included meaningful interaction with Christians in each of these six evangelism styles. Many first connected through friendships with Christians who invited them to come meet our church family. As they visited, other Christians built relationships with them, allowing them to meet people who shared how Christ had made a difference in their lives, and in whom they could see a genuine Christian love and service for others. Over time, they began having more serious spiritual conversations, with Christians who loved them enough to ask about their faith, talk about Christianity, and try to answer any questions they had. Eventually, they made their own decision to be baptized into Christ and begin a life of faith. All of this happened not through one person, but through the unified efforts of a church working tougher, encouraging people to follow God.

You may not be the apostle Paul, and you may not be an extrovert or have all the answers. Do not worry, you are not alone in that—but you are still part of Christ's evangelistic mission. Reflect on your own evangelism personality and how you can contribute to the larger goal of Christian outreach. And then, put your natural talents to work for Christ. Remember, this is not just *your* mission; this is *God's* mission, and we all join him in making it *our* mission, as a church family. As we all serve together, God uses his people to bring souls to him.

Discussion Questions

1) When you picture someone who is good at evangelism, what type of person comes to mind? What characteristics do they have?

2) What do the "church as a body of many members" passages (Rom. 12:4-6; 1 Cor. 12:12-27; Eph. 4:11-16) tell us about the church's evangelism mission, whether you think you have evangelistic talents or not?

3) Which of the evangelism personalities do we usually consider best for evangelism? Why? Do we need to be careful about giving the impression that those are the only ways to contribute to evangelism?

4) Another example of the "share-my-story" style of evangelism is the apostle Paul. (Actually, Paul had characteristics of all six evangelism personalities!) Some examples of Paul "sharing his story" can be found in Acts 22:1-21; Acts 26:1-23; Galatians 1:13-24; Philippians 3:4-9; and 1 Timothy 1:12-16. Why did Paul tell his story so often? What did he hope it would accomplish?

5) If we have not had a dramatic life turnaround like Paul, might we be tempted to think we do not really have a story to share about Christ changing our lives? Do we all have ways Christ

has changed our lives, even if they do not seem "dramatic"? Do people need to hear those stories also?

6) Does your church family have people who fit in every evangelism personality type? Why might that be important for local church outreach?

7) Do we sometimes view evangelism as something we have to do all by ourselves? Why? What are the weaknesses of that mindset?

Personal Reflection

1) Which evangelism personality type am I? Or do I fit in two of the types? Or more?

2) Which evangelism personality type would I like to grow more in my life?

3) Am I using my God-given personality to contribute to the church's evangelistic mission? What should I be doing that I have not been doing lately?

4) What are some of my faith stories that non-Christians may need to hear, to help them see the goodness of Christianity? Some questions to help you think: How is my life different and better because Christ is in it? What are some difficulties I have faced, and how has my faith helped me? Look for opportunities to share those things!

Endnotes for Chapter 5

[1] You find the theme of "evangelism personalities" in several books on evangelism, but I think most would agree the concept has been popularized by the writings of Mark Mittelberg. Mittelberg himself gives credit for the "evangelism personalities" concept to a sermon by Bill Hybels which Mittelberg found to be a personal "aha" moment (*Building a Contagious*

Church: Revolutionizing the Way We View and Do Evangelism (Grand Rapids, MI: Zondervan, 2000), 156-7).

Mittelberg writes about evangelism personalities in several of his books: *Building a Contagious Church,* 156f; *Becoming a Contagious Christian* (written with Bill Hybels (Grand Rapids, MI: Zondervan, 1994)), 119-132, and this concept is the overarching focus of Mittelberg's 2021 book *Contagious Faith: Discover Your Natural Style for Sharing Jesus with Others* (Grand Rapids, MI: Zondervan, 2021).

[2] Will McRaney Jr., *The Art of Personal Evangelism: Sharing Jesus in a Changing Culture* (Nashville, TN: Broadman and Holman, 2003), 54

[3] Mittelberg, *Building a Contagious Church,* 157-8.

[4] Kevin Harney, *Organic Outreach for Ordinary People: Sharing Good News Naturally,* updated and expanded edition (Grand Rapids, MI: Zondervan, 2018), 90.

[5] John P. Bowen, *Evangelism for "Normal" People: Good News for Those Looking for a Fresh Approach* (Minneapolis, MN: Augsburg Fortress, 2002), 204.

[6] Even Mittelberg, for example, who popularized this concept, uses different lists, sometimes identifying 6 categories (in *Becoming a Contagious Christian*) and in his latest book narrowing it down to 5 (*Contagious Faith*).

[7] This list is modified from Mittelberg's *Building a Contagious Church,* 158. For clarity's sake and my own wording preferences, I changed three of the descriptions: I changed "Confrontational" Style (#1) to "Direct," a change Mittelberg also made in *Becoming a Contagious Christian*; I changed "Testimonial Style" (#3) to "Share-My-Story" Style, similar to a change Mittelberg also made in *Contagious Faith*; and I changed "Interpersonal" Style (#4) to "Relationship-Building."

[8] Christopher B. James, *Church Planting in Post-Christian Soil: Theology and Practice* (New York: Oxford University Press, 2018), 17-18, 22-23.

[9] David Kinnaman and Gabe Lyons, *unChristian: What a New Generation Really Thinks About Christianity ... And Why It Matters* (Grand Rapids, MI: Baker Books, 2007), 41-66.

[10] Mittelberg, *Contagious Faith,* 66.

Chapter 6

Effective Evangelism
in Post-Christian Culture:

Getting Our Motives Right

"In everything, therefore, treat people the same way you want them to treat you, for this is the Law and the Prophets." —Matthew 7:12

The Struggle for Authenticity in Evangelism

From beginning to end, Christianity is about genuine love for others. Notice this theme in several key Christian foundations:

- **God's love for us** is the motivation behind Jesus coming to Earth and God receiving us back to him (John 3:16; Luke 15:11-32).
- Jesus said the **first and second commandments** are loving God with our entire being and loving others as ourselves (Matt. 22:36-40).
- **Jesus' sacrificial death** shows us what true love looks like, and Christians are to follow his example and show sacrificial love for others (1 John 3:16).
- **The world will recognize us as Christians** when we love one another as Jesus loved us (John 13:34-35).

- Christians are supposed to **love others even when it is difficult**, such as loving our enemies, being patient, and showing kindness in all circumstances (Matt. 5:43-48; 1 Cor. 13:4-7).

Christianity begins with God's love for us, and it results in his love flowing through our lives toward others.

Since Christianity is founded on genuine love for others, it was surprising when one study revealed that non-Christians do not always see that in us, and part of it has to do with evangelism. In the book *unchristian*, David Kinnaman and Gabe Lyons share research about how non-Christians perceived Christians. While some of the negative stereotypes were expected, one of the more disappointing findings was that many non-Christians viewed Christians as insincere [1]—especially when it came to sharing their faith. People reported feeling "targeted" for conversion, and many doubted whether Christians genuinely cared about them as individuals. As a Christian, that is difficult to hear. We want to share the gospel, but people sometime perceive those efforts as being targeted by Christians with insincere motives. How can we do better so that our evangelistic efforts are received as genuine?

While part of the problem may be that unbelievers misunderstand Christian motives, the fact is that Christians sometimes struggle with their own motives in evangelism. They want to encourage faith, but they do not want to feel like they are targeting non-Christians either, and they do not want to feel like they have ulterior motives or hidden agendas. Unfortunately, some people think of evangelism as trying to "sell" someone on something they do not really want—like a high-pressure sales pitch for a used car or a timeshare—and most of us do not feel right about that. After all, we do not like it when we feel like people have agendas in talking to us, so we do not want to be those people either.

Let us start with some good news that will help us with motive concerns: evangelism is *not* about pressuring someone into making decisions they do not want to make. It is not about trying to debate or manipulate people into accepting something they do not want. Remember, people must make their own heart decisions between themselves and God, and at best we can simply be encouragers and teachers. And once we remove that incorrect view of evangelism from our minds, there is more good news: we *can* share our faith with healthier motives, which will make all our interactions more authentic.

It is important to acknowledge two reasons why Christians must be intentional about purifying their evangelism motives. *First, Christians need sincere evangelism motives because motives matter to God.* God wants our motives to be right in evangelism, just like everything else in our faith. Christianity teaches the importance of both doing the right things and doing them *for the right reasons.* For example, in Matthew 6:1-7, Jesus rebukes the religious leaders for their prayers and their giving. Someone might ask, why would Jesus criticize praying and giving? The problem was their motives. They were praying and giving for show, to impress other people and draw praise for themselves, not to honor God. Their motives missed the mark, and Jesus made it clear: God is not pleased by outward acts that lack inward sincerity. The same idea is found in 1 Corinthians 13:1-3. There, Paul writes that even if Christians give all their possessions to feed the poor or surrender their bodies to be burned, if their motives are not based in genuine love, "it profits me nothing." Our evangelism efforts will not be pleasing to God unless we develop the right motives.

Second, Christians need sincere evangelism motives because in our skeptical, post-Christian culture, motives matter. As Kinnaman and Lyons explain, "A generation reared in a marketing-drenched world is quick to sniff out what they believe to be the underlying motivations and superficialities."[2] People in our culture tend to be suspicious of others' intentions, especially when it comes to religion, and they will withdraw if they sense an underlying agenda. They do not want to be impersonal targets for someone else's checklist. They do not want to feel pressured to do something that someone else wants them to do. They do not want to be treated like a project. And frankly, neither would we. Our evangelism efforts will not be effective—especially in post-Christian culture—unless we develop the right motives.

When sharing the gospel, we aim to encourage others to follow Christ, and we want to do it with genuine motives. That is the focus of this chapter: the feeling in our culture that Christians have ulterior motives has led several post-Christian evangelism authors to encourage healthier, more authentic motives in evangelism and in relationships. What are the appropriate evangelism motives, and how can we build them into our lives?

Identifying Some Wrong Motives

We must first admit that there can be insincere motives in evangelism, so we can identify them and avoid them. Many of the less sincere motives for evangelism stem from the same mindset problem mentioned in earlier chapters: it is possible to make someone else's salvation more about us than about them. For example, some Christians may approach evangelism as a kind of spiritual scoreboard, viewing someone's conversion to Christ as a "notch in their belt" that shows how good a Christian they are. That perspective can lead Christians to view non-Christians in an impersonal way, only interacting with them in hopes they will become a Christian and thus show that they themselves are good Christians.

Another way this problem can show itself: some Christians see evangelism as something that depends entirely on whether they say and do the right things to "convince" someone to believe. That perspective can lead Christians to badger non-Christians, searching continually for the "right words" that will lead to a conversion, subconsciously fearing their own personal "failure" in evangelism. Or yet another way this might happen: Christians sometimes feel anxiety for others' salvation—which in some ways is understandable, because we realize the seriousness of souls and eternity—and it can lead Christians to pressure non-Christians inappropriately, trying to calm the anxieties we feel for them. If we make someone else's salvation more about us than about them, we are misunderstanding that person's own responsibility before God, and we may be tempted to interact with them in ways that are inappropriate and counterproductive.

To help Christians keep better perspective, some writers remind us to be aware of how we speak about evangelism.[3] We do not want our terminology to give the impression that someone else's salvation is more about our actions than their choices, with overtones of objectivization or sales marketing or manipulation. For example, let us not say that we "converted" someone, as if we talked them into Christianity against their will; rather, we should rejoice with them that they decided to follow Jesus. We should be careful speaking about evangelism "strategies," language that might sound impersonal or self-serving; instead, let us pursue ministries that reach out in the name of Christ. We never want to talk as if non-Christians are objects or targets, and we do not want to give the impression that we are trying to manipulate anyone.

A few years ago, some Christians were telling me about recent baptisms at their congregation. As they described it, their congregation began an evangelism strategy to send cards to people who were hurting in order to convert them. I listened kindly and I appreciated their desire to reach out with the gospel, but inside I felt worried about those new Christians. What would those new Christians think when they became part of the church family and heard more about this evangelism strategy? I worried they would look back at their conversion and feel manipulated. They might decide that the church had not really cared about them as it originally appeared, that they were merely the objects of a strategy, and wonder if they had made a mistake. I hope I was wrong, and perhaps the Christians who described it to me simply used terminology that sounded more impersonal than they meant. The conversation reminded me that we must be careful how we speak about outreach. After all, it is good to send cards to people who are hurting, and it is good to reach out to people with the gospel. Both are worthy Christian activities, and both can be done with sincere motives. But if we describe those activities as if they are an impersonal "strategy" that only intends to "convert people," such language can give the wrong impression, both to Christians sending the cards and to the non-Christians who receive them. Motives matter, and how we speak about our actions makes a difference in clarifying our motives. If we speak about evangelism in appropriate ways, it will help both Christians and non-Christians understand our motives properly.

Sadly, some evangelism approaches seem manipulative and impersonal, and I believe most people can sense that dynamic when it happens, causing them to pull away. As we described in Chapter Two, we must strive to be committed to evangelism without being anxious about evangelism. Evangelism anxiety comes from the belief that another's salvation depends entirely on us, making it more about our actions than their choices, and shifting our motives in an unhealthy direction. If we remain committed to evangelism without being anxious, it guards us from self-centered motives and helps us interact with non-Christians in more respectful, appropriate ways.

Having acknowledged that it is possible to have incorrect motives in evangelism, we then ask the next question: how can we build healthier motives for relationships and evangelism?

Our True Motive in Relationships

What should our motives be in relationships? Jesus was clear about the first and second commandments of Christianity. The first is to love God with our entire life, and the second one has to do with how we treat others:

"You shall love your neighbor as yourself." —Matthew 22:37-39

In the Sermon on the Mount, Jesus also said this about relationships:

"In everything, therefore, treat people the same way you want
them to treat you, for this is the Law and the Prophets."
—*Matthew 7:12*

God wants us to treat people with sincere love, the way we would want to be treated. Whether it is a first meeting or a long-time acquaintance, we want to treat others with respect, kindness, and a sincere desire for their good. When we do this correctly, it follows the example of God's love for us. Does God love us only when we follow him? No!—God's love for us is unconditional. While God's salvation is conditional—and he has given us those conditions—God's love for us is unconditional. Even if we turn our backs on him, God still provides rain and sun to help the crops grow, for both the evil and the good (Matt. 5:45). God does not offer insincere love for others, and neither should we.

Here is one way Christians can internalize this principle: *We want to be a blessing to the lives of those around us, whether they ever become Christians or not.* That may be worth repeating to ourselves a few times. We want to meet people and show a sincere interest in their lives. We want to build relationships and encourage others. And yes, whenever faith topics come up, we want to encourage them in that also, in hopes they will follow Christ and receive all his blessings. But even if they never give their lives to follow Christ, we will still show love. Jesus did good to others (Acts 10:35), encouraged people to receive salvation (Luke 19:10), and showed sincere love even if people were not following God (John 8:7-11; Mark 10:21). Like Jesus, our hope is that others will give their lives to follow God; but also like Jesus, we will keep showing love to them even if they do not.

Having a mindset of loving and blessing others is a great way to shine God's light, and it is an authentically good motive for our interactions and relationships. When sincere love for others is present, I believe most people recognize our actions—including our evangelistic encouragements—as authentic, and that makes a big difference in how they receive us. We do not

97

show kindness to people only because we see them as targets or prospects for conversion. We do not talk to people only if they will become Christians and then drop them if they do not. We do not make other people's salvation more about us than them. Our motives are much deeper and much better. Pray that God would give us a sincere love for others, and may we strive to be a blessing to those around us. People will notice.

Other Biblical Motives for Evangelism

Genuine love for people should be the primary motive in all our relationships and interactions. Once we have internalized that motive, we then notice other biblical motives that make evangelism an authentic part of our lives.

First, a biblical motive for evangelism is an overflow of something we love. "Overflow" is one of my favorite images of evangelism. When we have a genuine faith and love for God, it will naturally overflow in our relationships and conversations. That is what happens when we are passionate about something. When you love a sports team or a video you saw online or a new restaurant or a new exercise program, you find yourself naturally talking about it with others, saying things like, "check this out, you would love it."

After Jesus healed the demon-possessed man in Mark 5, the man asked if he could come with Jesus back across the Sea of Galilee. But Jesus had a better plan in mind. Jesus told him: *"Go home to your people and report to them what great things the Lord has done for you, and how He had mercy on you"* (v. 19). And in verse 20, that is exactly what the man did: *"And he went away and began to proclaim in Decapolis what great things Jesus had done for him; and everyone was amazed."* The man had been healed, and he could not help but share with others how it changed his life.

The overflow principle means that we can build authentic evangelism motives by deepening our own faith and love for God. As our faith grows and we truly recognize what great things God has done in our lives, we will naturally want to share that with others. It will overflow in our relationships and conversations in an authentic, natural way, just like anything we are passionate about. When we love God, we find ourselves telling people and encouraging them to give their lives to God also.

Second, a biblical motive for evangelism is obedience to God. Jesus handed his evangelistic mission to his church, and he commands us to share the gospel with all nations (Matt. 28:18-20). However, some post-Christian evangelism writers caution against obedience as our only motive for evangelism,[4] and I understand their concern. They worry that reducing evangelism to an obligation will bring about joyless, impersonal evangelism efforts, as if we are merely trudging through an assigned checklist. Further, if we only see evangelism a form of personal obedience, we may be tempted to make the results more about us than about the non-Christian and tend toward pressuring or badgering, as we discussed above.

To avoid those pitfalls, it is wise to balance our desire to obey God with other biblical evangelism motives, such as sincere love for others, a desire to bless people's lives, and genuine overflow of something about which we are passionate. But at the same time, we must acknowledge that obedience is still a biblical motivation for sharing the gospel, and it is one that we sometimes need. Sometimes the desire to obey God helps us push through our fears of discomfort or rejection. It helps us have the conversation about faith when the topic comes up, give the invitation to church, or tell someone we are praying for them. We do not want obedience to be our only motive for evangelism, but sometimes a desire to obey God helps us take evangelistic steps we would not take otherwise.

Third, a biblical motive for evangelism is sharing something good. In 2 Kings 7, the Aramean army laid siege to Samaria, and the city was starving. Four hungry lepers at the city gate decided to go to the Aramean army to beg for food. When they arrived at the enemy camp, they found that the army had fled, leaving behind food, money, and clothing. After eating, drinking, and hiding some of the treasure, the lepers said to one another: "We are not doing right. This day is a day of good news, but we are keeping silent" (2 Kings 7:9). Notice their thought process: we have discovered something that will help everyone live, and it is not right to keep silent about it.

Do we believe that the gospel is "good news," as the word *gospel* means? What makes Christianity a message of good news? Here is a list for starters: peace in Christ, strength for life's struggles, forgiveness of sins, hope for eternity, life transformation, a spiritual family, relationship with our Creator who loves us, the best possible path for our life, a path marked by what is good and right. We could go on! Jesus said he came to give us "abundant life" (John 10:10). Paul said our faith "holds promise for the present life and also for the life to come" (1 Tim. 4:8).

When we truly see that Christianity is good for our lives and our eternities, we feel like those lepers: it is not right to keep silent about this. We want to share it with others, so they can be blessed. When we see people struggling in sin or with the burdens of life, we need to point them to Jesus, the one who can truly save and help. Of course, they will have to decide for themselves, but our motivation is a sincere one: this is something good that has blessed my life, I would love for you to experience it also.

Sharing the Gospel, with Sincere Motives

For effective evangelism in our culture, Christians must cultivate the proper *evangelism motives*. Our relationship motives should always be sincere, but that is especially important in a skeptical culture where people are sensitive about being pressured or treated as an object for someone else's agenda. It is important to clarify in our minds: we do not show kindness to people just because we want to "convert" them. Evangelism is not about manipulation or pressuring people to accept something they do not want. Their decision to follow Jesus is just that: their

100

decision. May we never make it more about ourselves than about them. We are encouragers and teachers, at best.

Following the example and teaching of Jesus, our motive in relationships is to show genuine love toward others, whether in a single conversation or an ongoing friendship. We show love and kindness because we want to be a blessing to everyone God puts in our lives, whether they decide to follow God or not. As one writer describes it, these types of sincere relationships become "a means to minister to them, to enter their lives, and to demonstrate God's love tangibly to them. ... This divine love that we are to demonstrate is unconditional, unswerving, and unrelenting, giving but expecting nothing in return."[5]

When we love people the way God loves them, our sincere desire for their good allows the interactions to be genuine. Faith issues may well come up organically, as they tend to do in all genuine relationships, and when they come up, our motives in those discussions will be sincere: we love God and the blessings he gives his children, and we would love others to have those same blessings. Sincere love, sincere friendships, sincere conversations. Those are the types of relationships that tend to change lives—and often eternities—for the better.

Discussion Questions

1) Do some people only talk with you when they have an agenda? How does that make you feel?

2) Do you enjoy high-pressure sales, such as the stereotype of car sales or timeshare sales? Why or why not? Do Christians sometimes have the misperception that evangelism is like high-pressure sales tactics or manipulation? How can we avoid that misunderstanding?

3) Do you think Christians sometimes struggle to have sincere motives for evangelism and relationships? Why?

4) Are there some wrong motives for evangelism? How can we avoid them?

5) Does God only show love to those who obey him? Are there examples in Jesus' life of showing sincere love even toward those who were not obeying God? (Some passages to consider: Mark 10:21; John 8:1-11; Luke 15:1-2.) What example does that give Christians for our relationships with non-Christians?

6) What are some good, biblical, authentic motives for evangelism?

7) Is obedience to God a proper motivation for evangelism? Why might we need to balance obedience with other biblical motivations? How does the obedience motive help us share our faith?

8) How can we interact with people, including looking for opportunities to share the gospel with them, without feeling like we have an agenda?

9) Imagine you are door knocking in the community, inviting people to an upcoming church event (Vacation Bible School, for example) and talking to someone at their door. How might you talk with them in ways that show genuine love and a desire to bless their lives? What are some ways you could talk that would be pressuring or manipulative?

10) What are some blessings of Christianity that we want others to have for themselves?

Personal Reflection

1) Do I have a sincere love for others, whether they are Christians or not? How do I show that? How can I deepen my love for others? Pray that God would help us keep growing in this Christian quality.

2) What are some ways Christianity has blessed my life? If I reflect on those and deepen my thankfulness for them, will it help me be more evangelistic in my life? How?

3) What are my motives for sharing my faith? How can I purify my motives so my relationships can be fully sincere?

Endnotes for Chapter 6

[1] David Kinnaman and Gabe Lyons, *unChristian: What a New Generation Really Thinks About Christianity ... And Why It Matters* (Grand Rapids, MI: Baker Books, 2007), 69.

[2] Kinnaman and Lyons, *unchristian*, 68-69.

[3] For examples:

John P. Bowen, *Evangelism for "Normal" People: Good News for Those Looking for a Fresh Approach* (Minneapolis, MN: Augsburg Fortress, 2002), 20.

Rick Richardson, *You Found Me: New Research on How Unchurched Nones, Millennials, and Irreligious Are Surprisingly Open to Christian Faith (Downers Grove, IL: IVP Books, 2019)*, 172.

[4] For example: David M. Gustafson, *Gospel Witness: Evangelism in Word and Deed* (Grand Rapids, MI: Eerdmans, 2019), 65-66.

[5] Gustafson, *Gospel Witness*, 63.

Chapter 7

Effective Evangelism
in Post-Christian Culture:

Building Genuine Relationships

"Iron sharpens iron, so one man sharpens another."—Proverbs 27:17

The Path to Christianity in Less-Receptive Cultures

Some cultures are more receptive than others. In some societies, the people are interested in hearing more about Christianity, and thus more open to faith conversations and truth-seeking. For example, many countries in South America, Africa, and southern Asia currently fit this description. Christians can walk up and start a faith conversation, and almost anyone will be happy to discuss Jesus and his teachings. Christians can send flyers out to the community inviting people to learn about Jesus and many will show up. Christians can teach the Bible through television or radio programs and large numbers will listen and respond. Receptive cultures are more eager to hear the Christian message, and we need Christians in those places, sharing the gospel with as many as they can.

What about our current American culture? Do most people seem receptive, interested in listening to Christians and seeking truth? At best, our current American culture is a mixed bag in this regard. There are still people who are receptive and seeking God. There will still be some who respond after they receive a flyer in the mail or watch a devotional online. But there are many who are not receptive, and on average, non-Christians in our current culture know less about Christianity and are less open to it than past generations.[1] As we noted in previous chapters, many non-Christians in our culture assume they already know what Christianity teaches and have decided they are against it.[2] Modern American culture is more secular, more wealthy, and more focused on entertainment than prior generations, leading to less interest in spiritual needs and lower receptivity toward the gospel.[3]

For one example of this shift, Christians have noticed a difference in the way people respond to door-to-door outreach. Prior generations of Christians speak of door-knocking as a primary, successful means of evangelism. Their efforts found many people willing to have a Bible study even if the evangelist was a stranger. Today, though, door-to-door evangelistic outreach is received far differently. Instead of finding receptive listeners, we more often find people who are fearful of being scammed or victimized, or simply annoyed at the interruption. No soliciting signs are common throughout neighborhoods today. I am not against door knocking, and my experience is that good things still come from it, even if less frequently than in the past. We must simply be aware that most people will be untrusting and disinterested, so we must knock doors in a way that is respectful of people's space and time. Our culture is simply different, less receptive than it used to be.

So how do most people become Christians in post-Christian cultures? The statistics say that it most often happens through relationships. In recent years, studies have consistently found that around 65-75% of people who became Christians did so through a relationship with a Christian, such as a family member or a Christian friend.[4] I am surprised those percentages are not even higher. Why? Because we are a skeptical, suspicious culture, and when it comes to big life decisions, we usually listen to people we believe we can trust. If we do not know someone personally, it is going to take a while before we trust them, especially about something as important as our religious decisions.

Relationships are foundations of trust. When we have a genuine relationship with someone, it makes sense that they would be more receptive to conversations about faith and invitations to church activities. Thom Rainer's 2003 study found that 80% of unbelievers said they would visit a church if they were invited and accompanied by a Christian individual with whom they have a personal relationship. [5] Rick Richardson's 2019 survey of two thousand unchurched individuals found the numbers somewhat lower, but still significant: 51% said they would respond positively if a friend invited them to a church activity, and 55% if they were invited by family.[6] People sometimes ask where are the open doors in our culture, and this is a big one: inviting our friends and family is a big open door, encouraging people with whom we already have genuine relationships.

Here is what we learn from the studies mentioned above: personal relationships are an important pathway to Christianity! We see that pathway in the New Testament as well:

- In John 1:40-42, Andrew meets Jesus, and he immediately finds *his brother* Simon. Simon Peter becomes an apostle and a strong person of faith, and it started because his brother introduced him to Jesus.
- In John 1:43-51, Jesus meets Philip, who finds *his friend* Nathanael to bring him to meet Jesus also. Nathanael comes to believe in Jesus, and it started because his friend introduced them.
- In Acts 10:24, when Peter comes to meet Cornelius, he finds that Cornelius has invited *his relatives and close friends* to come hear God's message. They hear the message, and at least some of them—maybe all of them—were baptized (Acts 10:48).

- In Acts 16:30-34, the Philippian jailer takes Paul and Silas to his house so *his family* can hear about Jesus. They listen, believe, and are baptized into Christ.

Those passages show that personal relationships have always been a significant factor in the spread of Christianity. That principle feels even more important in a culture that is less receptive and less trusting of people they do not know—and for that matter, a culture that has fewer actual personal relationships as people spend more time online, keeping the world at a digital distance.

The importance of relationships in post-Christian evangelism teaches us at least two things:

1) *First, we need every Christian to be part of the church's evangelistic mission.* You will have relationships with people that other Christians will never meet, and vice versa. Your friends and family members will usually be more receptive to you than they will be to someone else. We need every Christian to actively encourage faith and offer invitations in their relationships.

2) *Second, building relationships with non-Christians is an important part of evangelism.* How can we do that appropriately and make it a bigger part of our lives? That is our focus for the remainder of this chapter.

Recommitting Ourselves to Relationship Building

As we have seen, personal relationships are important pathways for evangelism, especially in post-Christian culture. Yet, studies reveal that American Christians do not always have relationships with non-Christians. In one recent survey, 38% of professing Christians said they did not have a single non-Christian friend or family member. [7] Another study on Christian relationships observed that Christians tend to become more socially isolated from non-Christians over time. [8]

On one level, it is easy to understand how this happens. As we follow Christ, we find that non-Christians are simply going in a different life direction. We have different goals, we talk differently, we spend our time differently. It feels easier to spend time with Christians. Additionally, God wants Christians to spend time together, strengthening each other's faith through our examples and encouragement. It is understandable that we may spend more time with fellow Christians as our faith grows; however, recognizing the significance of personal relationships for evangelism, many writers encourage more balance in this area.[9] They recommend remaining close to Christians for spiritual support while also striving to develop meaningful connections with non-Christians, where Christ's light can best be seen. After all, Jesus said we are to be salt and light in the world (Matt. 5:13-16), and light does not make an impact unless it shines into darkness.

The New Testament gives us several good examples of building relationships with non-Christians. One example we noticed in Chapter Five is Levi (also known as Matthew). In Luke 5:27-32, Levi leaves tax collecting and becomes a follower of Jesus. He then hosts a reception in his house, inviting his tax collecting friends to come meet Jesus and the apostles. He was allowing relationships to be built, planting seeds for faith encouragement.

Jesus himself is a great example for us. Notice one reason the Pharisees criticized Jesus: "He receives sinners and eats with them" (Luke 15:1-2). Or as Jesus described their criticism in Matthew 11:19, he was called a "a friend of tax collectors and sinners." Jesus had friendly relationships with people who were sinners! Of course, he did not just spend time with them, he also encouraged them to follow God, as we see in Luke 5:31-32 and Luke 15:1, and he certainly did not let them be negative influences on how he lived. Jesus gives us an excellent example of spending time both with believers and with unbelievers, building relationships and looking for opportunities to encourage faith.

A Relationship-Building Way of Life

So how can we get more balanced in this area? *First, recognize that friendship with non-Christians is a good thing, as long as we do not allow those relationships to influence us negatively.* Some Christians struggle with this concept, because they worry that showing kindness to unbelievers might suggest approval of their sinful lifestyles. But kindness is not approval. Jesus showed kindness to sinners. Christians are supposed to be "kind to all" (2 Tim. 2:24), not only to people whose lives are right with God. Kindness is a fruit of the Spirit (Gal. 5:22-23), and we must show kindness to everyone God puts in our lives, whether they live holy lives or not.

We do not encourage unbelievers toward Jesus by ignoring them. Instead, they need to see God's goodness through relationships with Christians, in the way we treat them and the way we live. When the opportunity arises, they will hear us discuss what we believe and why (1 Pet. 3:15), and it will be better received in the context of a real relationship. Now, if a non-Christian tells us to get out of their lives because we are Christians and they do not appreciate our life message, then yes, we wipe the dust off our feet and keep going in life (Matt. 10:14). However, as Jesus' example shows us, we can continue friendly relationships with those who have not yet obeyed the gospel. In an increasingly secular culture, Christians must get better at showing kindness and friendship to unbelievers.

Second, keep the right motives in our relationships. Remember our discussion from the last chapter: we do not want to de-humanize relationships by seeing non-Christians merely as evangelistic projects. Instead, we build relationships with people out of a genuine love for God and others, hoping to be a blessing to their lives whether they become Christians or not. Faith issues may come up in conversation, as they tend to do eventually in all relationships, and we should keep our eyes open for those opportunities. We should also look for opportunities to invite our friends to church events. But our motives for friendship need to be sincere and real, even if they never respond positively to Christ. As we build relationships with unbelievers, we must keep the right motives in mind.

Third, develop the Christian quality of hospitality—an essential part of relationship building. Several verses encourage Christians to be hospitable, to other Christians and also to strangers. (Some passages to read: Romans 12:13; 1 Peter 4:9; 1 Timothy 3:2; 5:10; Titus 1:8; 3 John 5-8.) In a couple of those passages, we find that hospitality is a quality God expects from elders, implying this is a characteristic of Christian maturity. Hospitality invites someone into our home or into our lives, often sharing a meal while extending kindness and relationship. We may want to ask ourselves: who in our life can we invite to lunch or to coffee? Or is there someone we can invite to our home to eat dinner? To whom can we show more kindness and friendship? We should extend hospitality to our fellow Christians, but we should also show hospitality and friendship to those who are not yet Christians. Sharing a meal or coffee is a simple, great way to build relationships.

Cautions for Relationship Building

Since the focus of this chapter is on relationship building, we should add a few cautions of Christian wisdom. *First, keep your own faith strong, refusing to allow any relationship to negatively impact your faith.* If we allow another person to pull our lives in the wrong spiritual direction, then we have become "unequally yoked" in that relationship (as the King James Version translates 2 Cor. 6:14). If that happens, we need to be wise and distance ourselves appropriately. If someone is truly "bad company" spiritually (1 Cor. 15:33), we must not immerse ourselves too deeply in that relationship, lest we be tempted to speak, think, or act in ways that sin against God. We must show the appropriate measure of kindness and friendship without allowing others to weaken our faith.

We may need to consider our level of spiritual maturity in this relationship-building goal. One of our newer Christians at church, a young adult, told me he was still trying to grow in his faith and develop better habits, so he felt he was not yet ready to start building closer relationships with non-Christians. I thought that was wise. He is making his faith a priority, in hopes that one day he will develop enough Christian maturity to be the stronger spiritual influence in all his relationships. We must be wise and never allow relationships to pull us down spiritually.

Second, learn wisdom for handling awkward spiritual situations. When we spend time with people who are not yet Christians, whether at work, school, or over coffee, they will often say or do things that we know are not right in God's eyes. We must develop wisdom in managing those moments. Is it worth pointing out every time they say something wrong about religion? Should we call them out every time they say a curse word or criticize them for ordering a drink of alcohol? Can we show kindness in a way that does not show approval or support for things that are wrong? We must prayerfully develop wisdom to handle awkward spiritual situations, picking our battles, and trying to discern when to offer a word of encouragement and when to just keep showing kindness and patience, waiting for a more appropriate time.

Third, show wisdom in building relationships with people of the opposite sex. There is an appropriate distance that must be maintained in any such relationship. If we are married, for example, we do not need to get emotionally connected to someone else of the opposite sex. We can still be kind and have conversations about faith, but having one-on-one coffee trips or lunches is not the best course of action. The goal of relationship building is a good one, but we must maintain appropriate distance and be wise in how we relate to the opposite sex.

Fourth, show a genuine faith, while acknowledging our faith is not perfect. Our goal in relationships is not to pretend that everything in our life is perfect or that we never make mistakes. In fact, it sometimes helps non-Christians to see that Christians have struggles too. But we must not go to the other extreme and be hypocrites. Our lives will always fall short in some way, but a hypocrite is a fake—someone who claims to follow God but does not genuinely try to live like it. We never want to be fake. It may help a non-Christian to see that Christians are not perfect, but they should also see that we are sincerely trying to grow more like Christ. Let us strive for a *genuine* faith; imperfect, yes, but genuine. When we have a genuine, humble faith, Christ's light shines in our relationships.

Building Bridges for the Gospel

For effective evangelism in our culture, we need strong Christians *building relationships* with those who are not yet Christians. Our neighbors hear many things about Christians from social media or movies or television shows, and sadly many of those outlets produce negative impressions of Christianity. People need to meet a real Christian, someone who will be a blessing to their lives, and someone with whom they can discuss faith issues as the opportunity arises. Christians should not underestimate the impact it has on an unbeliever when they see a genuine Christian example.

We need more Christians striving to find the right balance in our relationships: maintaining close relationships with their church family while also building appropriate friendships with unbelievers. The more we build those relationships, the more natural pathways to Christ will be opened. Of course, not all our non-Christian friends or family will become Christians, but over time, some of them will. At the very least, we will be a blessing to them and God will work in their lives, giving them opportunities to draw closer to him. Personal relationships are the most common pathway to Christianity, especially in post-Christian cultures. We need more Christians building those relationship bridges.

Discussion Questions

1) Do you agree that the United States is currently a less-receptive, less-trusting culture?

2) Does it make sense that most people in our culture become Christians through personal relationships? Why? Where have you seen that in your own life or in your church family?

3) Why might Christians struggle to have friendships with those who are not Christians?

4) Does showing kindness to someone mean that we approve of everything in their life? What verses or biblical examples remind us that kindness is different from approval?

5) Do you agree that there is a "balance" we need to have in our Christian and non-Christian relationships? How can we keep strong Christian relationships, while also making sure we do not lose all contact with people who are not Christians?

6) Does building relationships with people mean I must become their best friend or spend all my time with them? What does that teach us about relationship building with those who are not Christians?

7) How can we best handle awkward spiritual situations when we are spending time with people who are not Christians? How have you managed some of these in the past? What can we learn about trying to do even better in the future?

8) Is there a difference in having an imperfect life and having a hypocritical life? How can people see that we are genuine—not perfect, and certainly not hypocrites, but genuine?

Personal Reflection

1) Who in my life is not yet a Christian? Do they see a Christian example in me? How can I be a better example to them?

2) Am I spiritually mature enough to be a good influence in my relationships with unbelievers? If not, how can I keep growing

in my faith? How can I make sure I do not let bad examples influence the way I think and act?

3) What can I do to build closer relationships with some of the non-Christians in my life? Is there someone I can ask to get coffee or have lunch sometime?

Endnotes for Chapter 7

[1] We highlighted this reality in Chapter Four. For another source that notes it: Will McRaney Jr., *The Art of Personal Evangelism: Sharing Jesus in a Changing Culture* (Nashville, TN: Broadman and Holman, 2003), 3-4.

[2] David M. Gustafson, *Gospel Witness: Evangelism in Word and Deed* (Grand Rapids, MI: Eerdmans, 2019), 5.

[3] Barna Group, *Reviving Evangelism: Current Realities that Demand a New Vision for Sharing Faith* (Ventura, CA: Barna Group, 2019), 12, 19.

[4] Several studies to note.

- Shawn D. Anderson, *Living Dangerously*. A nationwide survey found that 70% of Christians said there was a key individual who was influential in leading them to Christ. (Eugene, OR: Wipf and Stock, 2010), 28.

- Gary S. Comer, *Soul Whisperer: Why the Church Must Change the Way It Views Evangelism*. Points to a New England study of recent Christian converts, in which 71% said a relationship with a caring Christian friend was the most important factor (Eugene, OR: Resource Publications, 2013), 141. (Also see footnote on p. 141.)

- Barna Group, *Translating the Great Commission: What Spreading the Gospel Means to U.S. Christians in the 21st Century*. A 2018 Barna Research study of U.S. churchgoers (not just new converts) found that 19% became Christians through conversations with a Christian they knew personally, and many more (48%) as a result of relationships with their Christian family members. (Ventura, CA: The Barna Group, 2018), 22-23.

- Michael Green, *Evangelism in the Early Church*, rev. ed. England—another post-Christian culture—shows similar results: Green appeals to British surveys revealing that most new Christians regard a close relationship with a Christian as the most important factor in their conversion (Grand Rapids, MI: Eerdmans, 2003), 24.

[5] Thom S. Rainer, *The Unchurched Next Door* (Grand Rapids, MI: Zondervan, 2003), 232.

[6] Rick Richardson, *You Found Me: New Research on How Unchurched Nones, Millennials, and Irreligious Are Surprisingly Open to Christian Faith* (Downers Grove, IL: IVP Books, 2019), 61f.

[7] Barna Group, *Reviving Evangelism*, 10.

[8] David Kinnaman and Gabe Lyons, *unChristian: What a New Generation Really Thinks About Christianity … And Why It Matters* (Grand Rapids, MI: Baker Books, 2007), 130.

[9] Some examples:
- Kinnaman and Lyons, *unChristian*, 130.
- Barna Group, *Reviving Evangelism*, 10.
- Timothy Keller online article, commenting on Michael Green's *Evangelism in the Early Church*. Tim Keller, "Evangelism in the early church." Online article. Accessed March 13, 2022, at https://www.redeemer.com/redeemer-report/article/evangelism_in_the_early_church.

Chapter 8

Effective Evangelism
in Post-Christian Culture:

Commitment to Faith Conversations

"So he [Paul] was reasoning in the synagogue with the Jews and the God-fearing Gentiles, and in the marketplace every day with those who happened to be present."—Acts 17:17

The Need for Words in Evangelism

So far in this study, we have noticed that a patient, relationship-building mindset is usually a more effective way to share the gospel in our culture. In our context, people often start further away and need more time to process decisions to come to Christ, requiring patience; and people are less trusting of those they do not know, requiring investment in personal relationships. However, there is an important addition we must make to the patient, relationship-building mindset: at some point, words must be spoken for someone to become a Christian. The Christian message is fundamental in evangelism.

No one has ever become a Christian without words. Notice the importance of words for developing faith in Romans 10:14,17:

How then will they call on Him in whom they have not believed? How will they believe in Him whom they have not heard? And how will they hear without a preacher? (v. 14)

So faith comes from hearing, and hearing by the word of Christ. (v. 17)

These verses indicate that hearing God's word is a necessary step towards becoming a Christian. If you are a Christian, at some point you heard the gospel. Maybe it was from a preacher in a worship service or a youth minister in a Bible class; maybe it was from a parent or grandparent; maybe it was from reading the Bible someone gave you. However it happened, the word of God was a significant part of your decision to become a Christian.

Even after you heard the word of God, you might have needed someone to give you a word of encouragement, stirring up your intention to obey the gospel. Some people know about Jesus, but need a friend or family member to ask caring questions like, "Did you ever become a Christian? Have you thought about it? What is holding you back on it?" That type of conversation is not necessarily teaching something new, but it simply encourages someone to act on what they already know. Oftentimes a simple, encouraging conversation is what people need, helping them resolve to do what they know they need to do.

Since words are needed for people to become Christians, we must not make the mistake of thinking that a good example is enough by itself to lead others to Christ. A good example is important, and there are people who became Christians because they saw a Christian example and started asking questions about their faith. However, even in those circumstances, a good example could only spur on conversations, and the gospel was then shared in words. An authentic Christian example is essential, but we must also be ready to communicate words that encourage others to follow Jesus.

The Importance of Conversation in Our Culture

Are there certain types of communication that are more effective for sharing the gospel in our culture? In a post-Christian culture, skeptical of religion and sensitive to anything that might sound judgmental, there is "an overall cultural resistance to conversations that highlight people's differences."[1] Thus, people in our culture tend to withdraw if they feel Christians are sharing their beliefs too strongly, especially if they do not have a personal relationship with them. In that type of context, sermonizing our beliefs to others or trying to debate religion is usually not as well received. Many Christians find that instead of an immediate gospel presentation or memorized speech, a more-effective first goal should be authentic conversation. As one writer says about sharing faith in post-Christian culture: "two-way conversation is more productive than one-way presentation," and "the ministry of conversation is the most important single way that the faith's meaning is communicated."[2]

I like that phrase, "the ministry of conversation," and that will be our focus in this chapter and the next. Simply having conversations about faith can indeed be a "ministry." When someone shares their thoughts with us in conversation, we usually think about their words again later, especially if it involves matters as important as our faith. Conversations often plant seeds in our minds, motivating us to think or act differently in the future.

Conversations can impact our lives, and looking for opportunities to have faith conversations is certainly biblical. We notice in the New Testament that there is a difference between sermons and conversations, and that both types of communication had their place in sharing the gospel, depending on which was more appropriate for the moment. In Acts 17:22-31, Paul shares a sermon in Athens, after being invited to share his beliefs at the Areopagus. He spoke and people listened, as expected from a sermon. But earlier in the chapter, Paul began his ministry in Athens not through sermons but through conversations. Notice Acts 17:16-17:

Now while Paul was waiting for them at Athens, his spirit was being provoked within him as he was observing the city full of idols. So he was reasoning in the synagogue with the Jews and the God-fearing Gentiles, and in the market place every day with those who happened to be present.

We learn several things from Paul in that section of Scripture. First, it hurt him to see the city full of idols. May we feel that same hurt when we see the world consumed by things that pull their souls away from God. Second, we learn from Paul's response to a culture consumed by the wrong things: he went to the people and began having conversations. Notice the word "reasoning" in verse 17. What is the difference between "preaching" and "reasoning"? Reasoning implies a two-way conversation. Asking questions, listening to the answers, responding in return, all the things that make up genuine discussion. Paul was not preaching *at* people, he was talking *with* people. There is an important difference, one that we need to learn ourselves.

How important is conversation for effective evangelism in our culture? Rick Richardson's *You Found Me* is a study of American churches across the denominational spectrum that grew through conversions (as contrasted with transfer growth from people who were already professing Christians coming into their congregations). One of his discoveries was that church members sharing their faith story and having religious conversations is a predictive factor for churches to have high conversion rates. [3] In other words, his study found that when churches have more people engaging in religious conversations in their lives, it results in more people coming to Christ. That should not be a surprise; the more we discuss faith with others, the more hearts will be stirred up to think about their relationship with God, leading some to decide that they want to follow God themselves. Faith conversations are an important way to share our faith, so let us keep our eyes open for opportunities to discuss faith with others!

When Did Jesus Have Faith Conversations?

Some people debate when is the best time to have spiritual conversations with non-Christians. Should it be in our first conversation? Or should we wait until we get to know them better? Or does it depend on circumstances? Notice some examples from Jesus' ministry, and see if we can draw any conclusions:

- *Sometimes Jesus discussed faith in the first conversation, because the other person brought it up.* In John 3:1-2, Nicodemus comes to Jesus asking faith questions. Notice that Jesus did not run from the conversation. He did not say, "let's wait until we get to know each other better and then we will talk about faith later." Jesus was happy to have the conversation. We also notice that Jesus did not push Nicodemus away with the conversation, patiently allowing Nicodemus to find the courage to act on his faith, which happens later in John's gospel. (See John 7:45-52; 19:30-32.)

- *Sometimes Jesus began a conversation about other matters, and then Jesus brought up faith as the conversation evolved.* In John 4:1-30, Jesus talks with a Samaritan woman at the well. The woman notices Jesus' kindness, asking about it (v. 9), leading Jesus to discuss faith issues. This produced a longer faith conversation, after which the woman leaves to tell others what she had seen and heard (vv. 28-30).

- *Sometimes Jesus simply offered friendship in the first conversation, and faith issues naturally arose in the conversation without Jesus bringing it up.* In Luke 19:1-10, Jesus meets Zaccheus and offers to eat with him. As they walk together, Zaccheus brings up faith matters, confessing ways he wants to repent and follow God. Again, Jesus is happy to have the conversation, which no doubt continued at Zaccheus' house.

- *Sometimes Jesus simply showed love and kindness in the first interaction, and he did not bring up faith issues until later conversations.* In John 9:1-12, Jesus gives sight to the blind man but does not discuss faith issues with him. Later, when they meet again, they discuss faith and Jesus encourages the man to believe in him. We see the same sequence in Luke 17:11-19, in which Jesus heals the lepers, but only discusses faith issues when one of the lepers comes back to thank him.

Is there any pattern we can discern in Jesus regarding faith conversations? Sometimes Jesus discussed faith in his first interaction with others and sometimes he waited until a later time; however, it is notable that Jesus always showed love, kindness, and friendship in his first interactions with people, which laid the groundwork for potential faith conversations. As he showed genuine love and interest toward others, sometimes faith issues arose and sometimes they did not. Jesus knew when it was appropriate to have a faith conversation and when it was best to wait. Even if we do not always know the perfect time to speak about faith matters, here is what we can take away from the example of Jesus: *show genuine love and interest in every interaction, and seek wisdom in deciding when to discuss spiritual issues.* Sometimes that will be the first conversation, sometimes it will be later conversations. But whenever the door opens for faith conversations, walk through it. Commit yourself to having the conversation, in hopes that it can encourage others closer to God.

There is a key word in that last paragraph for growing in our own "ministry of conversation:" *wisdom.* Colossians 4:5-6 uses that word in describing how we should interact with those who are not yet Christians:

Conduct yourselves with <u>wisdom</u> toward outsiders, making the most of the opportunity. Let your speech always be with grace, as though seasoned with salt, so that you will know how you should respond to each person.

How might we need wisdom in faith conversations? As we interact with others, we discern whether it is the right time to discuss faith or not. We discern whether we should bring up the topic, and if so, how best to do it authentically. When faith issues do come up, we discern whether the other person seems genuinely interested, and how much to say. Although we may initially feel deficient in such conversational wisdom, it will grow over time as we regularly engage in faith-based discussions. Wisdom is an important part of faith conversations, and it is a quality that can be developed, through prayer (see James 1:5) and practice.

Following the example of Jesus, may we show love and kindness to everyone we meet, and keep our eyes open for opportunities to have faith conversations. We will not always know the right time to bring up faith matters, but we want to try our best when the moment seems appropriate. We will never say the perfect thing every time, either, but we will grow in wisdom the more we have these discussions, and God can use our (imperfect) words to draw people closer to him.

What Attitude Did Jesus Show in Faith Conversations?

Those examples of Jesus' conversations also highlight an important Christian mindset for us to learn. As we noted, Jesus showed love to people, and at the same time he was looking to share God's truth. Is it possible both to show love and share God's truth? Not only is it possible, but it is Christlike, and it is essential. As Jesus spoke to people, he shared God's truth in such a way that people knew he cared about them. That is the perfect balance Christians are seeking, about which Paul wrote in Ephesians 4:15:

> *But speaking the truth in love, we are to grow up in all aspects into Him who is the head, even Christ,*

What a great goal for our interactions with others: "speaking the truth in love." It is possible to be so focused on sharing the truth that people do not think we genuinely care about them. Sadly, such approaches have left non-Christians feeling that Christians are judgmental and uncaring, only wanting to tell others how wrong they are. On the other hand, it is possible to be so focused on love that we are afraid to help people know and follow God's truth. Such approaches have left non-Christians ignorant of God's plan for their lives or feeling that the decision to follow Christ must not really be that important.

To help us think through the dangers of forgetting truth or forgetting love, I have shared an imaginary conversation below, and three different directions the conversation could go. If you are using this book in a Bible class or small group, it might be good to let two people role-play the parts for each of the three options and then ask the class what went wrong or right after each conversation. If you are just reading it for yourself, I hope you will picture the conversations in your mind, reflect on the pros and cons in each one, and consider how you might have a similar conversation in your own personality.

CONVERSATION OPTION # 1
(two high school friends sitting in the park after school)

Friend 1: "Since I consider you a friend, can I ask you a serious question?"

Friend 2: "Sure, what is it?"

Friend 1: "Do you go to church anywhere?"

Friend 2: "Yeah, I go to the Great Oaks Church of Christ. Why do you ask?"

Friend 1: "I have been thinking a lot about God lately. When I was little, I went to church a few times with my grandparents. My grandparents still go to church there, but my parents and I really have not gone anywhere for a long time. I never became a Christian or anything, and now I just feel far away from God. I know I cannot go to heaven if I am not close to God, but I do not really know what to do about it."

Friend 2: "Well, I know you are a really good person. I saw you help that girl who dropped her books today. And if anyone as nice as you is not going to be in heaven, then I do not think anyone will be there. You may not feel close to God, but I think you are closer to God than I am. Just keep being who you are, and I know God will take care of the rest."

Friend 1: "Thanks, that makes me feel a lot better."

Pause and reflect: What do you think about that conversation? What went wrong, and what should have happened instead? How might passages like John 14:6 (below) speak to how that conversation needed to be different?

> *Jesus said to him, "I am the way, and the truth, and the life; no one comes to the Father but through Me." —*John 14:6

CONVERSATION OPTION # 2

(two high school friends sitting in the park after school)

Friend 1: "Since I consider you a friend, can I ask you a serious question?"

Friend 2: "Sure, what is it?"

Friend 1: "Do you go to church anywhere?"

Friend 2: "Yeah, I go to the Great Oaks Church of Christ. Why do you ask?"

Friend 1: "I have been thinking a lot about God lately. When I was little, I went to church a few times with my grandparents. My grandparents still go to church there, but my parents and I really have not gone anywhere for a long time. I never became a Christian or anything, and now I just feel far away from God. I know I cannot go to heaven if I am not close to God, but I do not really know what to do about it."

Friend 2: "Well, you better do like I did and get baptized. Right now you are lost because you are not a Christian. And you better tell your parents to get their act together and start going to church, because they are being a bad example."

Friend 1: "Do not get me wrong, my parents are really good people. I did not mean to say that they are bad people."

Friend 2: "It does not matter how good they are. The Bible says that we are all sinners, and everyone who is not a Christian will face God's judgment when life is over. They need to change, and you do too."

Friend 1: "Well, maybe I will talk to my grandparents and see if we can start going to church again."

Friend 2: "How do you know the church your grandparents attend is a good church? The Bible is clear that not everyone teaches the truth, so their church might be full of false teachings. You need to check their teachings next to Scripture first, and you may need to be ready to take your grandparents and go somewhere else."

Friend 1: "Well, I will talk to them and we will decide what to do."

Friend 2: "Well, you better decide quickly. Your life could end at any second."

Friend 1: "I do not really want to talk about this anymore."

Friend 2: "Okay, sure. It is only the most important topic of your entire life. We should just ignore it."

Friend 1: "You are being really mean."

Friend 2: "I am just trying to talk some sense into you before it is too late."

Friend 1: "I do not need your help. I am leaving!"

Friend 2: "Fine, leave! But if you decide to get your life right, I can pick you up for church Sunday!"

Pause and reflect: What do you think about that conversation? What went wrong, and what should have happened instead? How might passages like 2 Timothy 2:24-25 (below) speak to how that conversation should have been different?

The Lord's bond-servant must not be quarrelsome, but be kind to all, able to teach, patient when wronged, with gentleness correcting those who are in opposition, if perhaps God may grant them repentance leading to the knowledge of the truth.
—2 Timothy 2:24-25

CONVERSATION OPTION # 3
(two high school friends sitting in the park after school)
Friend 1: "Since I consider you a friend, can I ask you a serious question?"
Friend 2: "Sure, what is it?"
Friend 1: "Do you go to church anywhere?"
Friend 2: "Yeah, I go to the Great Oaks Church of Christ. Why do you ask?"
Friend 1: "I have been thinking a lot about God lately. When I was little, I went to church a few times with my grandparents. My grandparents still go to church there, but my parents and I really have not gone anywhere for a long time. I never became a Christian or anything, and now I just feel far away from God. I know I cannot go to heaven if I am not close to God, but I do not really know what to do about it."
Friend 2: "Why don't you come to church with me this Sunday?"
Friend 1: "I have never been to a church of Christ before. What are the differences between all the churches?"
Friend 2: "Well, I cannot speak for other churches, but I know in our church we try to just follow Jesus, and we try to be undenominational Christians who follow the Bible."
Friend 1: "That sounds pretty good to me. So, are you a Christian?"
Friend 2: "Yeah, I became a Christian a couple of years ago. I asked my youth minister some questions one night after church, and then we had a Bible study together about what it means to be a Christian. I

committed to repent of my sins and then I was baptized to have my sins washed away. It was the best decision of my life. I know I am not perfect, but I am trying to live for God. And the Bible promises that Christians have forgiveness because of what Jesus did on the cross. So have you ever thought about becoming a Christian?"

Friend 1: "Yeah, I guess I have been thinking about it lately. I know a few things about Jesus, but I am not sure what I would need to do to be a Christian."

Friend 2: "Well, what if we talk to my youth minister and we can start having Bible studies together? That way you can ask questions and make your own decision. Do you want to come to church with me Sunday, and we can talk with him? I am happy to pick you up and we can go together."

Friend 1: "Sure, that sounds great! What time do you want to pick me up?"

Pause and reflect: What do you think about that conversation? What did you like or not like? Did it have better outcomes than the first two? Why?

What are your overall reactions to those three conversations? I think most people would say that the first conversation attempts to show love but fails because it does not show truth. The Christian was more concerned about making their friend feel better and told them things that do not agree with Scripture. Most would say the second conversation attempts to show truth but fails because it does not show love. Everything the friend said *might* be true, but it is said in such an unkind way—it is intentionally over-the-top, I hope no one would really talk like that!—that we cannot imagine anyone would want to listen to it. The third conversation is probably not perfect either, but it gives an example of pursuing both truth and love, while also showing wisdom to encourage the other person one step at a time. What pros and cons do you personally see in those conversations? How would you have the conversation differently in your own personality?

Like Jesus, we want to speak the truth in love, seeking wisdom as we encourage faith through our conversations.

The Commitment to Faith Conversations

For effective evangelism in our culture, Christians must learn the importance of having *faith conversations.* In this chapter, we have established a few basic foundations about the "ministry of conversation." First, conversations are important! Conversations cause us to think, and they can make a positive impact on our future, especially if someone is encouraging the right things. Second, we should follow the example of Jesus in how we approach people. Like Jesus, show genuine love and kindness in every interaction, and seek God's wisdom in deciding the appropriate time to discuss religious matters. Third, we should follow the example of Jesus in bringing the right attitude to religious conversations, speaking the truth in love. Truth and love are both essential if we want to help others draw closer to Christ.

If nothing else comes out of this chapter, let it be this: *let us commit ourselves to having faith conversations when the opportunity arises.* Do not shy away from the conversation. Do not run from it. If we all recommit ourselves to simply talking about faith more regularly with others, the statistics we mentioned earlier in the chapter tell us that more people will become Christians from that practice alone. [4] And that makes sense, because having faith conversations was an important way to share the gospel in the New Testament also, as we see in passages such as Acts 17:17, 1 Peter 3:15, and Colossians 4:5-6.

Let us recommit ourselves to having faith conversations as the opportunity arises!

In the next chapter, we will discuss ways we can get even better at having faith conversations. I pray it will help us feel more confident and ready when these opportunities arise, and I pray that God will use our conversations to bring souls closer to him.

Discussion Questions

1) Is a good Christian example enough by itself to bring people to Christ? Why or why not? What do Romans 10:14 and 10:17 say about the need for words in coming to Christ?

2) What is the difference between preaching and conversation? Do you see both in the ministry of Paul? What about in the ministry of Jesus? What other passages encourage Christians to be ready to discuss faith when the opportunity arises? (See 1 Peter 3:15; Colossians 4:5-6.)

3) Do you agree that people in our culture usually respond better to conversation than debating or sermonizing? Why or why not?

4) Does an effective faith conversation always have to teach something new? What are some ways we can simply encourage someone to act on what they may already know about Christianity?

5) Did Jesus talk to people about faith in every "first conversation" he had? Can you give an example of Jesus waiting to discuss faith in a later conversation? Why might he do that?

6) Do we always know when we should or should not talk about faith issues in a conversation? How can we try to decide?

7) Why is "wisdom" such an important concept for having faith conversations? In what ways do we seek wisdom while talking to other people?

8) Do you agree that many Christians—and maybe many churches also—struggle to show both truth and love in their

interactions with non-Christians? How does the example of Jesus help us?

Personal Reflection

1) When I became a Christian, who spoke or shared the words that helped me learn about Christ? Who has spoken words to encourage me to follow what I already knew to be right? What did they say, and how might I be able to do that for someone else?

2) Does my personality naturally lean toward "truth" in talking with others, or does it naturally lean toward "love" in talking with others? What can I do to make sure I show both truth and love in my conversations?

3) Have I had a time when there was an opportunity for a faith conversation, but I felt myself shying away from it? Why did I do that? What can I do better next time a similar opportunity arises?

Endnotes for Chapter 8

[1] Barna Group, *Reviving Evangelism: Current Realities that Demand a New Vision for Sharing Faith* (Ventura, CA: Barna Group, 2019), 48.

[2] George G. Hunter, III, *The Celtic Way of Evangelism: How Christianity Can Reach the West ... AGAIN*. 10th Anniversary ed., rev. and updated (Nashville, TN: Abingdon Press, 2010), 105.

[3] Rick Richardson, *You Found Me: New Research on How Unchurched Nones, Millennials, and Irreligious Are Surprisingly Open to Christian Faith* (Downers Grove, IL: IVP Books, 2019), 137.

[4] Richardson, *You Found Me*, 137.

Chapter 9

Effective Evangelism
in Post-Christian Culture:

A Toolbox for Faith Conversations

"Conduct yourselves with wisdom toward outsiders, making the most of the opportunity. Let your speech always be with grace, as though seasoned with salt, so that you will know how you should respond to each person."
—Colossians 4:5-6

A Desire to Do Better

Chapter Eight focused on the importance of having faith conversations with the people God brings into our lives. Jesus' ministry included faith conversations. Paul's ministry included faith conversations. We need as many Christians as possible engaging in the "ministry of conversation," encouraging others closer to Christ, in both truth and love, one step at a time.

Many Christians admit that they need to get better and more comfortable with faith conversations. This reality is highlighted in statistics we first mentioned in Chapter Two. One Barna Research study found that Christians are among the *most likely* to feel tension in having conversations with people who believe differently from them.[1] Another study found that 56% of professing Christians had two or fewer conversations about faith with a non-Christian during the previous year.[2] Why would Christians feel so much tension about having faith conversations with people who believe differently? And why would Christians have so few faith conversations with non-Christians? One problem is that, in addition to a fear of how people may react, many Christians also worry they will "fail God" in some way if they do not say the perfect thing at the perfect moment, so they just avoid the conversation altogether.

Should we avoid faith conversations since we do not always know the right thing to say? Of course not. In fact, it helps to acknowledge that our conversations will never be perfect. We will often wish we had said something differently. The answer is not to hide from the conversations; the answer is to pray that God will use even our imperfect conversations to help people think more about their soul and their relationship with God. God will keep working in their lives, even after our imperfect conversations. And more good news: the more we engage in faith conversations, the better we will get at the wisdom of "knowing what to say."

The main goal of the last chapter was to recommit ourselves to having faith conversations; the main goal of this chapter is to keep getting better at it. To help us grow in this area, we will present a "toolbox" of ten principles for having faith conversations in our post-Christian culture. As we make these principles a bigger part of our conversations, we will gain experience and wisdom, and we will get more comfortable talking about faith with those around us. It will never be perfect, but we will learn how to have faith conversations in our own personality, and God will use those conversations to bring souls closer to him.

Principle #1: Remember it is conversation, not preaching or debating.

There is a difference between preaching, debating, and conversation. Preaching is one-way communication. God uses it for good things, in its appropriate context. Debating is two-way communication, but it is a battle of ideas, and it is often competitive. God can use debating for good things also, in the right context, and when one debates in a Christlike manner. What we are encouraging for post-Christian interactions is not more preaching or more debating, though those have their places; we are encouraging more conversation.

Remember that conversation is a dialogue, implying two-way communication. Like any conversation, we speak, share our thoughts, and we invite the other person to speak and share their thoughts also. Many people will withdraw or get defensive if they sense we want to preach at them or debate them. Our goals in conversation are to discuss faith, hoping to stir up their thoughts toward spiritual things, and looking for the next step they need to take toward God (as we will see in Principle #8 below).

Principle #2: Ask questions.

One of the best ways to have faith conversations comes from a simple, non-threatening conversation principle: asking questions. Questions show that we care about people and have an interest in their lives and thoughts. Jesus was great at asking questions. Some of the many questions Jesus asked in his ministry: "What is written in the Law? How does it read to you?" (Luke 10:25-26). "Who do people say that I am?" (Matt. 16:13). "Do you believe that I am able to do this?" (Matt. 9:28). "Do you want to go away as well?" (John 6:67). Jesus was great at asking questions, stirring up thoughts, and showing that he cared about what the other person had to say.

Evangelistic Christians in the book of Acts were also good at asking questions. Philip started a conversation with the Ethiopian eunuch, asking, "Do you understand what you are reading?" (Acts 8:30). Paul explained to his listeners how he came to believe in Jesus, and then asked, "King Agrippa, do you believe the Prophets?" (Acts 26:27).

When we ask questions, we invite conversation and show interest. "Do you 'go to church' anywhere?" "What is your faith background?" "Have you ever visited with churches of Christ before?" "What did you think?"

"Were you ever baptized?" "Have you ever thought about it?" Those types of questions produce meaningful faith conversations.

Many Christians find that questions are a simple way to have faith conversations, in a sincere, non-threatening way. Keep your eyes open for opportunities to ask questions, showing that you are interested in people and where they are in their faith.

Principle #3: Listen.

If we are going to ask questions and have conversations, we must be willing to listen to the other person. Have you ever talked with someone who did not really listen? You probably felt like they did not really care about you, and you probably felt ready to just end the conversation and talk to someone else instead.

Listening shows genuine Christian love, communicating to people that they are valued and worth our time. James 1:19 reminds us to "be quick to hear, slow to speak and slow to anger." Those are good principles for relationships, and they are good principles for conversations as well. If you want the other person to know you care about them and their thoughts, be a listener. Ask questions, share your thoughts, but listen to theirs also.

Principle #4: Do not try to correct everything.

When we talk to people who have a different faith background or no faith background, they may have misunderstandings about God and the Bible. If you are asking questions and listening to their thoughts, you are likely to hear many things that you know are incorrect when compared to the Bible.

What should we do? Correct everything they say? If we are not careful, we will sound critical and condescending, as if we know everything and they do not. That is a good way to make someone defensive and quickly end any future opportunities. Would you want to talk with someone who felt the need to correct everything you said? Remember that listening kindly does not mean we agree with everything. You have heard things in sermons or classes at school with which you did not agree. You have had conversations with people, listening respectfully to their viewpoints, even if you did not agree with them. Listening does not mean agreement; it simply means we are showing kindness.

On the other hand, it is a conversation, and it is perfectly acceptable for you to share your understanding of things also. We must use wisdom to decide when it is worth sharing that we see things a little differently, and when we simply wait to discuss that issue another time. We must remember to be patient with people, trusting that God will continue working in their life, even after our imperfect conversation.

It helps to notice that sometimes Jesus overlooked certain errors to focus on bigger issues that he needed to address. Think of all that Jesus could have corrected in John 8:1-11, when the scribes and Pharisees brought the woman caught in adultery. Jesus could have listed the many things the Pharisees were doing wrong, as well as all the sins in the woman's life. Jesus did not avoid the issues, but he used wisdom in what most needed to be said in the moment and what would have to wait for another time. Consider also Jesus interaction with the rich young ruler in Matthew 19:16-22. Think of all Jesus could have listed when the man said he had kept all the commandments and asked what he lacked (v. 20). No doubt Jesus could have given an extensive list of his sins, but he focused on the biggest issue that needed to be addressed: the love of possessions was dominating the man's life. In fact, Jesus knew *everything* that was wrong in *every* person with whom he talked; he showed wisdom in deciding how much to correct in each conversation.

We are not failing God if we do not correct every single misunderstanding in a conversation. Following the example of Jesus, we are seeking wisdom in deciding when to overlook something and when to share that our understanding is different. And in those moments when we decide it is worth sharing a different understanding, we need Principle #5.

Principle #5: Share your thoughts kindly, not arrogantly.

No one likes a know-it-all, so be sure to speak kindly and humbly. We do not want to give the impression that we think we are "above" or "better" than anyone else. (Because we are not better than anyone else, we are merely sinful people who need Jesus talking to other sinful people who need Jesus.) We were blessed to be taught God's truth, and we want to share that truth in an attitude that honors God.

The right spirit for faith conversations is found in passages like 2 Timothy 2:24-25:

> *The Lord's bond-servant must not be quarrelsome, but be kind to all, able to teach, patient when wronged, with gentleness correcting those who are in opposition, if perhaps God may grant them repentance leading to the knowledge of the truth.*

Notice the attitude God wants from that passage: not quarrelsome, but instead kind, patient, and gentle even when giving a correction, with the goal of helping them come to know God and his truth. It is not enough just to say the right thing; we must also say things in the right spirit and with the right goals, as best we can.

Principle #6: Share how faith has impacted your life.

As we discuss faith and life with others, we will find moments when it is appropriate to share how faith has impacted our life. For example, conversations occasionally reveal that people are facing life challenges, such as cancer or family problems. What a great opportunity to let people know that we will pray for them, and if it is appropriate, even offer to pray together right then. Further, we could ask if they are a Christian and share how our own faith and church family have held us up in times of difficulty. Maybe invite them to visit our church assemblies or a small group Bible study to provide support as they go forward.

We all have stories to share about how God makes a difference in our lives. Sometimes Christians say, "I do not have a dramatic life story." That is fine, your stories do not have to be dramatic. But you *have* seen God's blessings in your life:

- You have seen God's strength in times of struggle.
- You have experienced the joy of salvation, either in becoming a Christian or coming back to Christ or both.
- You have seen the difference Christ made in someone else's life.
- You have seen how church family shows love to one another.

Think through the ways you have seen God's goodness in your life and be ready to share those stories when the appropriate moment comes.

Like the blind man in John 9, we do not have to be experts on theology or know the answer to every question. Many times, simply sharing what you have seen God do in your life is exactly what someone needs. Your experience is something you know better than anyone else, something you know is true. When people meet a Christian who has good things to say about God and their church family, it makes a difference. Keep your eyes open for opportunities to share how faith has impacted your life.

Principle #7: Seek wisdom in how much to say.

As part of the conversational "wisdom" encouraged in Colossians 4:5-6, when we discuss faith with others, we must try to discern how interested they seem in the conversation. Some people will appreciate a faith conversation. Others will not be interested. Still others will simply want to argue. As the conversation proceeds, seek wisdom in whether to continue the conversation and for how long.

One Christian lady at our congregation—who incidentally is very good at having faith conversations with people—recently made us laugh as she told about one of her conversations that took place in a grocery store. As she was telling another lady about our church family, she noticed the lady was slowly backing up with her shopping cart, physically moving further away from their conversation! The story was funny, but for the purposes of this principle, our Christian friend was wise enough to recognize that the lady did not want to have a lengthy conversation about faith or church. Our friend ended the conversation gracefully and continued shopping.

Many people are happy to discuss faith, especially when we discuss it the right way, so please do not think that everyone will react by backing away from the conversation! Our point: be wise during the conversation, deciding how much to say, how long we should discuss the topic, and when to bring the conversation to a close.

Principle #8: Encourage the next step.

What are the goals in our faith conversations? For one, we care about people and want to get to know them better. For another, we hope to stir up their thoughts about faith and God. For still another, we hope they will see us as a genuine Christian, someone who is real in our faith. For Principle #8, consider another important goal for faith conversations: encouraging them to take their next step toward God.

As the conversation proceeds, learn to ask yourself, "What is the next step I can encourage for this person to draw closer to God?" It may be helpful to remember the dominos illustration from Chapter Four about evangelistic patience. The person may be many steps away from God, but as you talk with them, try to envision what the next step might be. Do they need to visit a worship service or congregational event with you? Do they need to start reading the Bible for themselves? Do they need an encouragement not to give up on God or church? Do we need to exchange numbers or email addresses, so we can continue the conversation in the future? Do they seem interested enough to ask if they would like to start meeting for a one-on-one Bible study? Does the conversation "click" enough to ask if they would like to get coffee sometime and talk more?

Whatever you decide the next step might be, try to encourage it before the conversation ends. You will not correct everything in one conversation, especially in our culture, so it is wise to simply encourage that next step. "You should come visit our church family sometime, I think you would love it." "I know you have faced some difficult things, but I hope you will not give up on God." "I have enjoyed talking with you, how about we go get coffee sometime?" Remember, God will keep working in their life even after your conversation, but before the conversation ends, try to encourage them to take their next step toward God.

Principle #9: Close the conversation with kindness.

Colossians 4:5-6 tells us to have these conversations with "wisdom" and with "grace," which in my mind includes the way we end the conversation. Even if disagreements have emerged in your conversation, do your best to close the conversation with kindness. Let them know you enjoyed talking with them. Or encourage that next step at the end (Principle #8). Or let them know you will be praying for them. Or all the above!

We want people to see that Christians care about others, and as much as possible, we do not want the conversation to end with a feeling of conflict or enmity about our differences. We want their heart to be open to another conversation in the future, whether with us or with another Christian God puts in their lives.

Principle #10: Follow up.

If life allows it, do your best to follow up on the conversation at the appropriate time. If you told them you would pray for them, then after an appropriate amount of time, let them know you have been praying, and ask how things are going. If you said you would love to have them visit with your church family, bring them an invitation when there is an upcoming Friends and Family Sunday or a special church event. If you hoped to get together and talk more, reach back out and set a time to get together and keep the conversation going. Or, if you felt they did not seem interested in faith matters, just keep being a Christian friend in their life, and keep your eyes open for a future invitation or opportunity to talk again. (Some Christians worry that faith conversations will make things awkward with people in their lives. Determine that you will not act differently toward them, even if you worry they might feel awkward about it. Sometimes the "follow up" is that you will simply keep being a Christian friend who treats them with kindness.)

Not every faith conversation allows for a follow-up. You may have a brief conversation with a stranger and go your separate ways with no way to follow up. When that happens, simply pray and hand their future to God. He can do more with it than you can. But if the conversation does allow for a follow up, we still want to pray for God to work in their lives, and we also want to follow up in whatever way is appropriate.

Getting Better at Faith Conversations

The principles in this chapter are intended to help us think through having faith conversations in our own personalities. Even though these principles have been lined out as a "toolbox," they will still be applied from a sincere place: our genuine love for people, not trying to manipulate anyone, simply talking, listening, and encouraging. Other people must make their own faith decisions between themselves and God; we are simply trying to stir up their thoughts, be a good example of a genuine Christian, and encourage them to take the next step.

One more note that fits in the "wisdom" idea of Colossians 4:5-6: just like the advice in the relationship chapter, remember that male and female lines should be honored in our conversations. A married man does not need to be having deep emotional conversations with a female who is not his wife or asking if she would like to get coffee sometime to keep the conversation going. So be sure to keep appropriate boundaries in these conversations whenever they are conversations with the opposite sex.

For effective evangelism in our culture, Christians must *get better at having faith conversations*. Many Christians feel they do not know what to say, but the more we have these conversations, the more comfortable and effective we will become. If you have ever been door-knocking on a mission trip or around the neighborhood, going from house to house and having conversations with different people, then you know the feeling of starting out a little unsteady but eventually getting better at discussing faith matters in a sincere way that fits your own personality. In the same way, our faith conversations will never be perfect, but the more we have them, the more we will learn the "wisdom" and "grace" of Colossians 4:5-6, and the more we will help others think about their relationship with God. Let us commit ourselves to talking about faith when the opportunities arise, let us commit ourselves to getting better at it, and let us pray that God will bless our imperfect conversations to his glory.

Discussion Questions

1) Read Colossians 4:5-6. What does it say about our faith conversations with others? What words stand out to you?

2) The studies say that Christians are among the most likely to feel stress when having conversations with people who believe differently than us. Why do you think that is?

3) If we do not "say the right thing" to every issue in a faith conversation, have we failed God? What good things still come out of imperfect conversations?

4) What are some good, reasonable goals for us to have in our faith conversations?

5) Are we tempted to think that we do not really have a faith story worth sharing? Why? What are some different types of faith

143

stories we can share with others that might encourage them? (Hint: How have I seen God's goodness, guidance, or strength in my life?)

6) Brainstorm a list of possible "next steps" that we might want to encourage in a faith conversation. Is it difficult to limit ourselves to encouraging just one next step? Do you agree that encouraging just one next step is usually the best way?

7) Which of these 10 principles do you personally find to be most helpful?

8) Which of these 10 principles do you personally think is most difficult?

9) Are there any other faith conversation principles you have found to be helpful that are not on this list?

Personal Reflection

1) What faith conversation have I had recently? Which of the ten principles do I wish I would have applied to that conversation? How might that have changed the conversation?

2) What are some good things I have seen God do in my life? Can those become faith stories to share with others at appropriate times? Imagine what type of person may need to hear each of those different faith stories.

3) Which of the ten principles do I find most helpful? How can I apply it to future faith conversations?

Endnotes for Chapter 9

[1] David Kinnaman and Gabe Lyons, *Good Faith: Being a Christian When Society Thinks You're Irrelevant and Extreme* (Grand Rapids, MI: Baker Books, 2016), 44f.

[2] Barna Group, *Reviving Evangelism: Current Realities that Demand a New Vision for Sharing Faith* (Ventura, CA: Barna Group, 2019), 10-11.

Chapter 10

Effective Evangelism
in Post-Christian Culture:

Building an Evangelistic Church Culture (Part 1)

"By this all men will know that you are My disciples, if you have love for one another." —Jesus in John 13:35

The Importance of Culture in Evangelism

Culture[1] has been a buzzword in the business world for many years, and it is now a widespread concept. Here is one quote often heard among business leaders as the idea was popularized: "Culture eats strategy for breakfast." [2] What does that mean? It does not mean business strategy is bad; it simply means a group's "culture" is even more impactful than a strategy. Groups of people have their own group personality, their own group values, ways of making decisions, and ways of treating people. All those things contribute to the group's culture. And when the culture is right, organizations have their greatest potential to succeed.

Churches have cultures, too. Each congregation is made up of unique individuals, and that specific blend of people produces its own unique personality. And while every congregation should be striving to follow Jesus

Christ (Eph. 4:15), and thus aiming to be a genuinely Christian culture, there are also differences in each congregation's personality. Based on the people, the leadership, the history, and the emphasis (among other things), each congregation will have its own unique culture.

What does this have to do with evangelism? When a congregation's culture is healthy—focused on honoring God and helping souls come to him—it has the greatest potential for evangelism and spiritual growth. That is what the church is supposed to be: God's family, teaching, encouraging, and living out God's truth (1 Tim. 3:15). And when that happens, there is an organic feeling of God's goodness, encouraging everyone to draw closer to God.

Many Christians have experienced the impact of a God-focused group culture. You may have been on a mission trip, and the shared sense of purpose within the group produced spiritual growth in your life. Everyone was focused on glorifying God and helping others, and just serving alongside the team made you want to be closer to God. Or you may have spent time at a church camp, and the entire week of classes, songs, and Christian fellowship, alongside a group of people focused on God, made you want to take steps toward stronger faith. In my own life, mission trips to the Caribbean as a teen and church camp weeks as a college-age counselor played significant roles in building my faith. In those experiences, it was the committed spirit of the group that made me want to be more faithful. There was not a specific sermon or Bible class that stood out, nor did anyone directly tell me I needed to grow in my faith, but the God-focused and soul-focused nature of the entire group produced a desire to follow God more closely.

The church should be that way. And while the day-to-day and week-to-week nature of the local church cannot always replicate the intensity of a mission trip or church camp week, the church should be able to set a high spiritual tone, one that consistently encourages souls closer to God. In our songs, Bible teaching, fellowship, and genuine faith, our congregations can build a culture focused on God and souls, which will naturally motivate people to follow Christ.

A healthy church culture is an essential part of evangelism for another reason also: new Christians need a healthy church culture to grow in faith. Imagine that we begin practicing the things we have discussed in this book, and God blesses our efforts to bring souls to him. We pray for souls, build relationships with those who are not Christians, have faith conversations, encourage people to become Christians, and then over time we see souls decide to be baptized into Christ. After they are baptized, they will need to be connected to a church family, because that is God's plan for our Christian lives. Jesus established his church (Matt. 16:18) as a place for his people to worship, serve, and grow. When we enter a relationship with Jesus, we also enter a relationship with his people,[3] which is designed to help us grow and stay faithful to God.

You have probably seen people who decided to be baptized but the "connecting to a church family" step never happened. Perhaps they never made friends in the church or were disappointed the church family was not what they hoped it would be. Perhaps the church family never pulled them in and encouraged them to grow. Or maybe they simply turned away from their commitment to God, as Jesus said would sometimes happen (Matt. 13:20-21). Whatever the causes, when new Christians do not connect to a church family, the sad reality is most of them never grow in faith, and many simply turn back to the world. As people become Christians, we must help them meet and connect to God's people. Even if you personally grow to be effective in evangelism, you need a healthy church family alongside you.

For those reasons (and others), church culture is important for evangelism! As one writer describes it, Christians should aim for "the power of church-based evangelism" instead of relying completely on "the limitations of lone ranger evangelism."[4] Especially in a post-Christian culture, in which people are less trusting of others and many are wary of religious groups in general, unbelievers need to see the true goodness of a church family. A healthy church family will show people the goodness of following Jesus, and after they make their own decision to become a Christian, a healthy church family will help them keep growing in faith.

So how can we build an evangelistic church culture? In the rest of this chapter, we will discuss three qualities that will help any church family grow in their evangelistic effectiveness. In the next chapter, we will add three more, giving a total of six culture qualities for churches to develop. And while our congregations may never do any of these perfectly, growing these qualities will help us build church cultures that support and promote effective evangelism.

Culture Quality #1: Build a Culture of Loving People

The New Testament shows the important connection between church culture and evangelism. For example, look at what Jesus said in John 13:34-35:

> *A new commandment I give to you, that you love one another, even as I have loved you, that you also love one another. By this all men will know that you are My disciples, if you have love for one another."*

Notice especially verse 35; the world will know we are disciples of Jesus by the love we have for one another. That is a culture quality. Do we show genuine love for one another in the church? If we do, Jesus says the people around us will notice, and they will recognize us as his followers. Sadly, people do not always see a loving culture in churches. But when we get it right, it has an evangelistic impact: *"all men will know that you are My disciples."*

148

How can churches build cultures of truly loving people? This quality often begins with Christians deepening their relationship connections. Sharing meals together, spending time together, making time to talk about our lives—those simple building blocks of relationships lead to greater closeness. And while some relationship building will happen before and after worship assemblies, most churches find that they need additional times together for friendships to deepen. When we have church fellowship meals, we grow closer. When we have cookouts or board game nights or going to a ballgame, we strengthen our relationships. Cultures of caring begin with a commitment to spend time and share life together.

A group of Christians with close, spending-time-with-each-other relationships leads to evangelism opportunities. You often see this in teen ministries or college-age ministries. They begin with get-together events, building a sense of unity and togetherness, and the group develops a feeling of momentum and joy. They enjoy spending time with one another, and soon they invite their friends from outside the church to join them. After a while, those "spend time together" events lead to Bible studies, service projects, and other faith-building activities. Those who are already Christians grow in faith, and the friends they invite begin thinking about their own faith also, often leading some of them to become Christians. And it all started by building a sense of togetherness among a group of Christians.

We also build a culture of loving people by committing ourselves to the principle in Galatians 6:2: *"Bear one another's burdens, and thereby fulfill the law of Christ."* In every church family, there are Christians facing life challenges such as health issues, job losses, or family difficulties. Galatians 6:2 tells us that God does not want Christians to face life's burdens alone; he wants us to be there for one another. Therefore, Christians show love by sending cards, delivering meals, giving hugs, visiting and praying with one another—all the things you do when you show love to someone who is hurting.

As we become the loving church family God wants us to be, we naturally extend that "bear one another's burdens" mindset to others. Someone in our church family will have a close friend who is struggling, so we put her on our prayer list, and we show the same love to her that we show to each other. Someone in our church family will have a cousin who is sick in the hospital, and we show the same love to him that we show to each other. Prayer requests, prayer lists, sending cards, preparing meals, and genuine Christian love are important for living out our faith, and they are some of the best ways to reach out to our post-Christian culture. As Jesus said, *"By this all men will know that you are My disciples, if you have love for one another."*

Following the example of Jesus, let us build a church culture of loving people. People will notice, and it will produce evangelism opportunities.

Culture Quality #2: Build a Culture of Faith Commitment

We also see the connection between evangelism and church culture in the Jerusalem church of Acts 2:42-47. In verse 41, three thousand souls are baptized into Christ. And in the following verses, notice how connected they are to their faith and to each other:

They were continually devoting themselves to the apostles' teaching and to fellowship, to the breaking of bread and to prayer. Everyone kept feeling a sense of awe; and many wonders and signs were taking place through the apostles. And all those who had believed were together and had all things in common; and they began selling their property and possessions and were sharing them with all, as anyone might have need. Day by day continuing with one mind in the temple, and breaking bread from house to house, they were taking their meals together with gladness and sincerity of heart, praising God and having favor with all the people. And the Lord was adding to their number day by day those who were being saved.

With a group of Christians so committed to their faith and to each other, it is no surprise when verse 47 says, *"The Lord was adding to their number day by day those who were being saved."* They were committed to true Christian teaching (v. 42). They were committed to prayer and worship (v. 42). They were committed to spending time together (vv. 42,44,46). They were committed to helping each other (vv. 44-45). Unbelievers saw their commitment, and it led to a consistent stream of new Christians (v. 47). Sadly, people do not always see a culture of deep faith commitment in our churches. But to the extent we get it right, it has an evangelistic impact. People notice commitment, and for many, it produces an interest to see what is behind such a dedicated group of people.

How can we build cultures of faith commitment? Like the Jerusalem church in Acts 2, we want a church family that aims to make Christianity the focal point of our lives. In a culture led to believe that all Christians are hypocrites, unbelievers need to see authentic, committed faith. Here are a few suggestions for building this quality:

- *First, set a high spiritual tone.* Regularly remind people, "we know we will never be perfect, but we are sincerely trying to follow Jesus Christ with all our heart, soul, mind, and strength," just like Jesus taught in Mark 12:30. And then, with the church leadership leading the way, show lives that genuinely pursue that goal. Sadly, some churches look like little more than social clubs or entertainment venues, and they miss the big picture of glorifying God and encouraging souls to follow him. Keep reminding people that the goal is to honor God and put him first. Those who are truly seeking God will grow from that mindset and will be reminded that salvation in Christ is the most important thing in life.

- *Second, emphasize God's word in Scripture.* Teach the Bible, even the difficult, challenging parts. Encourage Christians to know it and follow it in their everyday lives. Teach why

Christians believe what we believe and why we practice what
we practice. There is a spiritual strength in the inspired word of
God; if we emphasize it, God will work through it to produce
spiritual growth. The Jerusalem church was "continually
devoting themselves to the apostles' teaching" (Acts 2:42).

Another of the Bible's great evangelistic church cultures
is the Antioch church in Acts 11, and one of the things
highlighted about this mission-minded church was their
"teaching culture." The church grew through "speaking the
word" (v. 19) and "preaching the Lord Jesus" (v. 20). And notice
this sentence in verse 26 about Paul and Barnabas: *"And for an
entire year they met with the church and taught considerable
numbers."* They were a teaching culture, and it produced
Christian commitment and evangelistic growth.

Remember what we said at the beginning of Chapter
Eight: no one becomes a Christian without words. When
unbelievers come to visit, make sure they hear Scripture taught
in worship. After all, if I were a non-Christian coming to a
Christian worship service, I would want to hear what the Bible
says and what Christians think about it. Make sure they hear the
Bible taught in Bible classes. Make sure they not only hear the
Bible taught, but hear it taught in a way that they know we
genuinely care about the listeners. Make sure people know that
the church offers personal Bible studies about Christianity. Part
of building a committed, evangelistic church culture is being a
"Bible teaching culture."

- *Third, find ways to encourage deeper faith.* Have an occasional
church-wide prayer emphasis, taking prayer requests from
friends in the community. Start a small group Bible study that
meets regularly, or a whole ministry of Bible study groups.

Have the entire congregation read through the Bible in a year. Find ways to focus on building stronger faith.

- *Fourth, make worship meaningful.* We do not want our worship to be stale or lifeless, but we also do not want it to be entertainment-oriented or performance-based. Worship should be both biblical and meaningful, and when we worship God his way (in spirit and truth, John 4:24) it builds deeper faith. Real, meaningful worship encourages everyone who is present to love God and follow him more closely. When unbelievers see that in us, it causes them to think about their own faith.

- *Fifth, stand with God, even when culture disagrees.* Do not listen to the voices who claim Christianity must change its teachings to survive. God knows what he is doing, he does not need us to change his word to please the world. He simply needs us to show a faith willing to "obey God rather than men" (Acts 5:29). People need to see that Christian convictions go deeper than just trying to give the culture whatever it wants to hear. Unbelievers will recognize true conviction, and it will challenge them to consider the source of such commitment.

No one is drawn to uncommitted faith. Christians and churches that seem lukewarm will never be a strong light for the gospel. And while it is difficult to keep an "on fire" feeling in our faith every single day, our churches can keep a steady fire going, as church families who encourage deep Christian commitment. In a post-Christian culture, people need to see a group of "all in" Christians, not perfect but authentically committed in their faith. That is the type of church family that makes unbelievers think about committing their lives to Christ also.

Culture Quality #3: Build a Culture of Inviting and Hospitality

A third way to promote an evangelistic church culture is to develop a culture of inviting and hospitality. As we have seen already in this book (see

Chapter Seven on Relationships), most people become Christians in our culture through personal relationships. And studies consistently show that most non-Christians say they would be open to visiting a church if they were invited by a Christian they know personally.[5] As we saw in that Chapter Seven discussion, this is one of the real open doors in our culture, if only we will invite our non-Christian friends and accompany them when they visit.

Create Inviting Opportunities

Since people in our culture are willing to visit if invited, churches should create regular opportunities for Christians to invite others. This can be done with both large-scale and smaller-scale events. The choice of these events will naturally vary by congregation, depending on the church's size, makeup, and interests. Here we offer some examples.

Large-scale events include the entire church family, and churches can experiment to find what types of events work best for their congregation. Large-scale events that provide inviting opportunities include Family and Friend Sundays, Vacation Bible Schools, multi-night Gospel Meetings, Bible Class Emphasis Sundays, seminars on Christian evidences, Homecoming weekends, church picnics, fall festivals. If churches plan several inviting events each year, it will provide regular opportunities to invite our non-Christian friends and family, and it allows the church to build relationships with those who visit.

Smaller-scale events are for smaller segments of the church family, such as activities for teens, young families, young adults, or seniors. Church camps, teen get-togethers, family picnics in the park, board game nights, and similar things are good smaller-scale events, giving Christians the opportunity to invite friends who might enjoy meeting Christians at similar life stages.

Regular invitation events also remind Christians to think about the non-Christians in their life, which fosters a culture of inviting for all the standard weekly Christian assemblies as well, such as Bible classes and worship times.

Create a Hospitality Culture

If we develop a culture of inviting, we must also develop a culture of hospitality, so that visitors will be greeted and welcomed when they visit. It would be very disappointing to invite a non-Christian friend to worship, only to find that no one else in the church welcomes them or gets to know them.

In Rick Richardson's book *You Found Me*, he identified several "predictive factors" that his research found to produce growth through evangelism and conversions. The number one "predictive factor" he found: a church's ability to show hospitality to the unchurched when they visit.[6] In other words, if *anyone* can visit with our church family—no matter how they look, no matter how little they know about Christianity, no matter their background—and be shown welcome, love, and kindness, Richardson's research says that quality will lead to people becoming Christians. And that makes sense. People need to see that Christians genuinely care about them and welcome them, allowing them to build relationships that eventually lead to real conversations about faith.

As several writers have noted, many unbelievers need to feel a sense of belonging among Christians before committing to Christianity themselves.[7] After all, if conversion to Christ really is a commitment to his church also, unbelievers need to see that our church family is a safe place, a group of Christians who will stand alongside them and encourage them after they make their own decision to follow Christ.

Churches usually require intentional organization to strengthen their culture of hospitality and welcome. Some churches have greeters ready at various places around the building to greet everyone who enters with a smile and handshake. Some churches have people looking through the auditorium to meet those who are new, before and after worship. Some churches use announcements to regularly encourage Christians to meet any unfamiliar faces that sit near them in classes or worship.

Hospitality is also shown by following up with those who visit. If a visitor trusts us enough to give their address, it is good to send a handwritten note to say thanks for visiting. Perhaps someone can deliver cookies to their house during the week, as a quick thank you for visiting. If someone has visited for a while, churches need people ready to ask if they would like to get together for coffee or lunch, to deepen the relationship and have a conversation about faith and next steps. Churches accomplish these goals in different ways, but if we want to have a culture of hospitality, we need to effectively greet those who visit and follow up with them also.

Show Hospitality in Worship

Another part of hospitality to unbelievers is making our worship times understandable to those who visit. If we are not careful, Christians may assume everyone understands our worship practices, without realizing that there are people in our assemblies who do not know what certain words or practices mean unless we clarify them. You might have had this experience yourself. I went to a funeral several years ago at a church with very different traditions and practices, and as the service went on, I felt like I was the only one who did not know when to stand, when to sit, or what to say. When that happens, we feel out of place or feel that this church does not really care if people from the outside understand what they are doing. If we do not make clear what we are doing, we miss an opportunity to let visitors know what we teach and practice, and why we think it is important.

In 1 Corinthians 14, Paul discusses several aspects of the Corinthian worship assembly, mostly about their use of the miraculous gifts of the Holy Spirit given through the apostles. Notice what he says in verses 23-25 about the need to be "visitor-conscious" in Christian worship assemblies:

Therefore if the whole church assembles together and all speak in tongues, and ungifted men or unbelievers enter, will they not say

that you are mad? But if all prophesy, and an unbeliever or
an ungifted man enters, he is convicted by all, he is called to account
by all; the secrets of his heart are disclosed; and so he will fall on his
face and worship God, declaring that God is certainly among you.

Paul writes that if an unbeliever was present in their worship—notice that unbelievers were invited to Christian worship times in the first century also—and people were speaking in tongues (languages) that listeners could not understand, the unbeliever would simply think the Christians were crazy. But if someone spoke in a language that was understandable, Paul says the unbeliever could be convicted by God's word and recognize that God is truly with this church family. Even if we do not have the miraculous gifts of the Spirit that Paul was discussing, there is still a worship principle to learn: we need to speak in ways that are understandable and meaningful in our worship times, at least for the unbelievers who are listening. If our worship is understandable, unbelievers have an opportunity to see what we believe and practice and be convicted by God's word.

Notice, however, that this is a "visitor conscious" emphasis, but not a "visitor driven" emphasis. There is an important difference. Some churches in the last few decades have responded to post-Christian culture by making assemblies entirely "visitor driven." This often includes changing the worship focus away from honoring God, instead making it an entertainment enterprise, focused on wanting visitors to "like it." But that shifts the entire focus of our faith in the wrong direction—away from God and toward people-pleasing.

People-pleasing attitudes tempt Christians to listen to culture more than to God, when God is clear that Christians should trust and obey him whether his word is popular or not (Prov. 3:5-6; Acts 5:29). In fact, many churches that jumped into a "visitor driven" approach have realized that approach led them in unfaithful directions. At least one of the major "visitor driven" churches did a self-study, concluding that their approach did not really build true disciples of Jesus, even if the attendance numbers had grown.[8]

The more faithful approach is to be "visitor conscious," not "visitor driven." When we are "visitor conscious," we are simply making sure our worship is understandable, speaking as if unbelievers are listening. (And they are, especially in a digital world where many churches livestream their worship!) For example, it is good to explain the meaning of the Lord's Supper before we take it together. It is also good for preachers to present "church language" in ways that even unbelievers can understand. When we speak in worship about people who are not Christians, we should speak in ways that are kind and never demeaning. By making our worship understandable and speaking as if unbelievers are listening, we help visitors see the goodness of God in our practices, helping them reflect on it for their own lives.

Christian worship assemblies have always been great opportunities for sharing the gospel. They are opportunities to invite others, opportunities to greet and build relationships with visitors, and opportunities to show the meaning and goodness of Christian worship and life. We should not make the mistake of being "visitor driven," but as "visitor conscious" Christians, let us build a culture of hospitality in our times of worship. Effective evangelism will result, even in post-Christian contexts.

Starting to Shape a Culture

For effective evangelism in our culture, Christians must recognize that *church culture* plays a vital role in sharing the gospel. The good news is that we can cultivate biblical qualities in our church families to enhance our outreach. In this chapter, we have explored three culture qualities that promote and support evangelism: *loving one another, deep faith commitment, and a spirit of invitation and hospitality.*

With God's help, let us strive to nurture these qualities in our churches! While no church will ever embody them perfectly, the more they grow, the more God's light will shine even brighter through us. In the next chapter, we will examine three additional culture qualities that contribute to more effective evangelism.

Discussion Questions

1) What does it mean for a group of people to have a "culture?" Whether it is a business, a friend group, or a country, what types of things make up a group culture?
2) Do you think each church has its own culture? What makes up the characteristics of a church's particular culture?
3) Do you agree that having a healthy church culture is essential for effective evangelism? Why or why not?
4) How can an evangelistic church culture be even more impactful than "lone ranger" everyone-do-it-by-themselves evangelism?
5) How can churches build cultures of loving people?
6) How can churches build cultures of deep faith commitment?
7) As part of a church's faith commitment, how can churches develop "teaching cultures" that truly teach God's word in Scripture? Do churches sometimes lose their focus on teaching Scripture? How?
8) Did unbelievers visit Christian worship assemblies in the first century? How does 1 Corinthians 14:23-25 help us answer that question?
9) How can churches build cultures of inviting and hospitality?

Personal Reflection

1) What can I do to help build a culture of loving people in my church family?

2) What can I do to help build a culture of deep faith commitment in my church family?

3) What can I do to help build a culture of inviting and hospitality in my church family?

4) Who in my life can I invite to an upcoming church event?

Endnotes for Chapter 10

[1] I am using the term "culture" in its popular sense. I am aware that sociologists would likely quibble with my descriptions and define the term differently in their field of study.

[2] Jacob M. Engel, "Why Does Culture 'Eat Strategy for Breakfast'?", Nov. 20, 2018. Forbes.com. https://www.forbes.com/councils/forbescoachescouncil/2018/11/20/why-does-culture-eat-strategy-for-breakfast/.

[3] For one example of this principle, 1 John 1:3 teaches that when we each have fellowship with God, we also have fellowship with one another.

[4] Mark Mittelberg, *Building a Contagious Church: Revolutionizing the Way We View and Do Evangelism* (Grand Rapids, MI: Zondervan, 2002), 22-23.

[5] Thom S. Rainer, *The Unchurched Next Door* (Grand Rapids, MI: Zondervan, 2003), 232.

Also: Rick Richardson, *You Found Me: New Research on How Unchurched Nones, Millennials, and Irreligious Are Surprisingly Open to Christian Faith* (Downers Grove, IL: IVP Books, 2019), 61f.

[6] Richardson, *You Found Me,* 16, 220-21.

[7] George G. Hunter, III, *The Celtic Way of Evangelism: How Christianity Can Reach the West ... AGAIN,* 10th Anniversary ed., rev. and updated (Nashville, TN: Abingdon Press, 2010), 105.

[8] G.L. Hawkins and Cally Parkinson, *Reveal: Where Are You?* (Barrington, IL: Willow Creek Resources, 2007), 3-4. A Willow Creek church self-study, which many, including their founding preacher, understood as a conclusive rebuke of the seeker sensitive evangelism model. This is one example of how

the "seeker-sensitive worship" model that was extremely popular for a time, is now just as likely to be seen as inadequate for effectively helping unbelievers develop a genuine, committed Christian faith.

Chapter 11

Effective Evangelism
in Post-Christian Culture:

Building an Evangelistic Church
Culture (Part 2)

"So then, while we have opportunity, let us do good to all people, and especially to those who are of the household of the faith."
—Galatians 6:10

Building An Evangelistic Church Culture, Part Two

When a church culture promotes and supports evangelism, it can be far more effective than "lone ranger" evangelists who do not have a healthy church family alongside them. In the last chapter, we introduced the importance of church culture for effective evangelism and highlighted three culture qualities that help churches best shine God's light. In this chapter, we will add three more culture qualities and share some final thoughts on building an evangelistic church culture.

Culture Quality #4: Build a Culture of Doing Good to All People

A fourth culture quality that promotes evangelism: build a church culture of doing good to all people. As Paul wrote in Galatians 6:10, *"So then, while we have opportunity, let us do good to all people, and especially to those who are of the household of the faith."* The last phrase of that verse teaches that we have a special responsibility to help our fellow Christians; but notice we also must do good to "all people," obviously including those who are not yet Christians.

Doing good to others was strongly connected with the rapid growth of early Christianity. As news of Jesus' ministry spread through Galilee and Judea, he was known not only for his teaching but also for healing people and helping people (Matt. 4:23-25). In fact, Peter would later describe Jesus' ministry as, "He went about doing good" (Acts 10:38). As Christianity spread throughout the Roman Empire, Christians followed the example of Jesus in helping others. The apostles healed people; the church contributed together to help the poor (Acts 11:27-30); and Christians such as Tabitha abounded "with deeds of kindness and charity which she continually did" (Acts 9:36). Church history further confirms that Christians had a reputation for compassion and assistance to those in need.[1] It is no accident that the Christian commitment to doing good was accompanied by rapid evangelistic growth as well.

How Doing Good Promotes Evangelism

How does doing good promote evangelism? There are at least three connections. First, serving others shows unbelievers the goodness of God in his people. Especially in a post-Christian culture in which many non-Christians have established negative impressions of Christianity, people need to see that Christians genuinely care about others, just like Jesus did. When people see God's goodness in his church, they are more open to hearing the life-changing message behind it. This is true for the people we serve and also for unbelievers who visit with our church families. When people see Christians doing good, it opens hearts for the gospel.

Second, doing good promotes evangelism by helping Christians build relationships with those outside the church. As we serve people and help people, we get to know them, and as we saw in Chapter Seven, personal relationships are the most common pathway to Christianity. Doing good in our communities allows Christians to keep connecting with people who live around us, providing potential relationship pathways for the gospel.

Third, doing good promotes evangelism by helping Christians think outwardly. If we are not careful, Christians can stay busy with all the (good) things to be done within our church families and forget our outreach mission. Serving others builds an outward-focused mentality and reminds us to be light in the world. When churches serve in their community, they find that the Christians who serve are suddenly more excited about having a faith conversation with a friend or inviting their friends to a church activity.

In these three ways, doing good for others has a strong connection to evangelism. In the spirit of keeping our motives right, we must also remember: we do good even if it does not lead to evangelism, because it follows Jesus' example of loving our neighbor as ourselves. However, as we serve others with the right motives, we find that doing good does indeed promote evangelism.

Do We Only Do Good if it Includes Evangelism?

Do churches have to choose between evangelism and doing good? In Rick Richardson's book *You Found Me*, he concluded that to grow through evangelism, churches must overcome the false idea that they must choose between doing good and sharing the gospel.[2] Other writers agree this is a problem,[3] suggesting churches often believe they must either be a "helping-people church" or a "gospel-teaching church," but not both.

Why might Christians struggle with that idea? Some churches believe that since everyone's biggest need is salvation, Christians should focus on evangelism instead of doing good. As a result, those churches often decide they will only do good for people if they allow us to share the gospel with them also. I understand the thought process—I agree everyone's biggest need is salvation, not just material assistance—and if Christians can share the gospel with someone as we serve them, that is even better. But it is still good in God's eyes to help people, even if it does not include evangelism in the moment. Further, if churches do not actively do good for others, even when it does not immediately include evangelism, I worry they are hindering their evangelism opportunities.

Consider the example of Jesus. Did Jesus only do good to people if he could share the gospel with them? In Chapter Eight, we looked at Jesus' interactions with others, noting Jesus' wisdom on when to have spiritual conversations. Jesus similarly used wisdom on when to share the gospel with the people he healed. It is true, sometimes Jesus talked about faith with people in the very moment he healed them. One example is the blind men in Matthew 9:27-30, with Jesus first asking them, "Do you believe that I am able to do this?" Other times, Jesus healed someone and waited until a later conversation to discuss faith. In John 9, Jesus gives sight to the blind man. It is not until later, after Jesus hears that the man was excluded from the synagogue, that Jesus finds him and discusses faith with him (John 9:35-39). Most conclusive for this discussion, sometimes Jesus healed people even though he never got the opportunity to discuss faith with them. One example is the ten lepers in Luke 17:11-19. Jesus heals them and tells them to go to the priests as commanded in the Law of Moses. Only one came back to thank Jesus, leading to a faith conversation. As for the other nine— it appears Jesus never got the opportunity to discuss faith with them. And yet he did good to them anyway.

Jesus believed in helping people even if it did not always immediately involve evangelism. Of course, Jesus' biggest concern was the soul, since he came "to seek and to save that which was lost" (Luke 19:10). Jesus was always eager to discuss spiritual matters. But he also believed in doing good, and he used wisdom in deciding the right time for faith conversations. Sometimes the moment was not appropriate for discussing the person's faith, so Jesus simply helped and waited for another opportunity to talk.

May we do the same: let us help people and serve people, keeping our eyes open for opportunities to share the gospel. But we should not force those moments in a way that might appear manipulative or insincere. If we are not careful, requiring people to hear the gospel to receive our kindness can leave people questioning Christian motives. Let me be clear: I am not saying we *cannot* or *should not* share the gospel as we serve others, because it is even better if we can also teach them about Jesus. I am simply saying we should show wisdom in deciding when it is appropriate and when it is not. That is what Jesus did.

Churches do not have to choose between evangelism and doing good. Jesus did both. The Christians in the New Testament did both. Some churches mistakenly think they must either be a "helping-people church" or a "gospel-teaching church," but God does not ask us to make that choice; God desires us to do both. Following the example of Jesus and the New Testament church, churches should teach others and serve others—each in their appropriate times—to best shine Christ's light into their communities.

How to Build a Culture of Doing Good

How can we build a church culture of doing good? Here are a few suggestions to help us begin:

- *Celebrate the good that is already happening.* Most congregations are already doing good in many ways: visiting nursing homes, sending cards to the hurting, delivering meals to sick, shut-ins, and families who are grieving. Do not let those things become "background." Regularly acknowledge those acts of service and publicly thank those who show Christ's love to others. When we celebrate doing good, the church will be motivated to multiply its good works.
- *Serve through the connections we already have in the community.* As we brainstorm how to do good in our community, consider

the connections that already exist. Are there teachers in our congregation? We could "adopt" their school, finding ways to encourage the teachers and students. Are there nurses in our congregation? We could provide treats for their team of nurses or provide needed items for patients on their floor. Do we have people who enjoy community activities? They could set up tables at community events, handing out treats and inviting people to learn more about our church family. There are so many possibilities! One of the best ways to begin is to reflect on our unique church family and serve through our existing connections.

- *Serve without enabling.* We want to serve others, but we do not want to enable people.[4] For example, those who work with the homeless and impoverished often warn against giving money handouts, saying it hinders people from making necessary life changes. I believe 2 Thessalonians 3:10 teaches a similar principle.

  Churches can serve without enabling by being intentional in their benevolence ministry. Make a list of "what we do" and "what we do not do" when people request assistance. Do we give money or pay bills for anyone who asks? Do we only pay bills for people who are part of our church family or have a personal connection to our church family? How often can people request assistance from the church? By establishing appropriate guidelines beforehand, churches can help in ways that are beneficial but not excessive, allowing people to maintain their own sense of personal responsibility. Some churches provide necessities like a food pantry and clothes closet, and for other requests they give a list of community services offered elsewhere. Some churches assemble "Blessing Bags" to put in their cars, with items like water and snacks for those in need on the side of the road.

No church has unlimited resources, so it is important to define what specific assistance the church will provide. Some churches embark on doing good without a plan and they end up feeling used and manipulated, along with the disappointing sense they did not really help anyone. It is better to have an intentional plan of service beforehand, allowing the church to serve without enabling.

- *Pursue relationship-oriented acts of service.* If we do good in a way that builds relationships, we provide the best potential for future evangelism opportunities. Regular visits to a nursing home allow Christians to build relationships. Offering homework help for local students or serving breakfast for first responders allow Christians to build relationships. Raking leaves for neighbors of church members allows Christians to build relationships.

  Now, it is perfectly fine to give money or pantry items to local causes, so I have no criticism when churches simply collect items and deliver them to a hospital or school. But even in those circumstances, you hope the church representatives making the delivery can build a small relationship with the group you are trying to serve. Relationship-oriented acts of service are great bridge-builders; if possible, find opportunities for those types of connections.

- *It is okay to start small!* You cannot do everything, and there will always be other churches doing more. It is not a competition. Find a starting place for service and begin. I recommend defining "what we can and cannot do" in your benevolence ministry first. Then start brainstorming your existing connections to the community and how you might show kindness through them. The goal is simply to do good for others, just like Jesus did. Start small, and God will bless and multiply it.

169

Culture Quality #5: Build a Culture of Team Evangelism

A fifth way to promote an evangelistic church culture is to emphasize "team evangelism." While it is good to teach "personal" evangelism—and much of this book has explored what Christians can "personally" do to share the gospel—we must also emphasize that evangelism is done together as a church family. When Christians see they have a place in the bigger outreach goal, with a team of Christians alongside them, they are more likely to engage in evangelistic activities.

How do we build a culture of team evangelism? First, emphasize that the Great Commission of Matthew 28:19-20 is a group command, not just for any one Christian on their own, but for the entire church:

> *Go therefore and make disciples of all the nations, baptizing them in the name of the Father and the Son and the Holy Spirit, teaching them to observe all that I commanded you; and lo, I am with you always, even to the end of the age.*

Jesus gave this command to his church for all generations— "to the end of the age" —and since it is a command to his church, we all share in the mission of teaching the gospel. Remind the church that we are an "outpost for the kingdom of God" in our community, with the group-wide task of shining God's light. Help everyone see the shared mission of the church, not just "your task" but "our task."

Second, emphasize that every Christian has a meaningful role in the church's outreach mission. The church is a body with many different parts and personalities, as we see in passages like Romans 12:4-5:

> *For just as we have many members in one body and all the members do not have the same function, so we, who are many, are one body in Christ, and individually members one of another.*

Christians have different talents, so we play different roles in the church's work, including evangelism. Churches would benefit from emphasizing the principles found in Chapter Five, about different evangelism personalities both in the New Testament and in the evangelism process today. We should celebrate all the evangelism personalities, not just the Peter and Paul types, but also the important roles of showing love to people, inviting friends, and welcoming visitors. We should avoid the impression that those who have Bible studies with others or seem to know all the answers are the "super-Christians," the only ones really fulfilling the Great Commission. We all have essential roles for effective evangelism, and we want every Christian to see how their unique contribution is meaningful.

Third, plan outreach events where Christians work together. Go in groups to serve the community. Host a Friends and Family Day or Vacation Bible School, encouraging everyone to invite friends and welcome visitors. Organize a Door-Knocking Saturday near the church building, sending people in groups to meet your neighbors and invite them to an upcoming event. Send mission teams to help churches in other areas with Vacation Bible Schools or community service. The more the church participates in outreach together, the stronger the spirit of "team evangelism" will grow.

While personal evangelism is vital, it is equally important to highlight how it connects with team evangelism—the collective mission of the church to reach souls. Keep teaching and emphasizing the church-wide aspect of evangelism. When Christians see their role in the bigger picture, they will be more motivated to take action, and it will strengthen the church's evangelism culture.

Culture Quality #6: Build a Culture that Keeps the Evangelistic Temperature High

Sixth, we can build a more evangelistic church culture by keeping the "evangelistic temperature" high in our congregation. This term, used in several evangelism writings,[5] refers to how much evangelism is on our minds and how actively we engage in it. When our evangelism temperature is low, we do not think about, pray about, or notice evangelism opportunities like we should. We raise our evangelism temperature by regularly reflecting on the importance of evangelism, and the higher our "temperature," the more focused we are on seeking gospel opportunities.

In a church context, regularly emphasizing the importance of salvation and outreach helps raise everyone's evangelistic temperature. Of course, overemphasis can lead to burnout or frustration, which is not the goal. Instead, we aim to keep evangelism appropriately on everyone's mind, helping us recognize opportunities to point others to God. Remember the conclusion of one study we have referenced a couple of times: the most effective way to foster evangelism is not through entertainment-driven services, but by motivating Christ-centered members to share their faith.[6] Keeping the evangelistic temperature high will inspire more Christians to push beyond their comfort zones and participate in outreach activities.

Ideas for Keeping Evangelistic Temperature High

So how can we keep the evangelistic temperature high in our churches? While regular outreach events and a high spiritual tone are key (which we mentioned in other sections above), here are a few additional ideas:

- *Celebrate baptisms and steps of faith.* In Luke 15, Jesus describes heaven's joy when a soul comes to God. If heaven is celebrating, we should celebrate too. When someone becomes a Christian, take baptism photos and feature them in the bulletin or on social media. Offer hugs and send cards. Have a special prayer for them at the next church assembly. When someone recommits their life to God or confesses sin, show support and love to them as well. Treat each step of faith as a significant event, helping the church focus more on salvation and evangelism.

- *Have regular evangelism classes or seminars.* Some Christians will want deeper training in sharing the gospel. Offer a Bible class on evangelism every year or two, studying evangelism in the book of Acts or a book about sharing our faith. Host occasional evangelism seminars. Regular training keeps evangelism on people's minds and equips them to share their faith.
- *Provide resources for evangelistic conversations.* Set up a "Conversations Table" in the church lobby with tracts, booklets, and Bible study materials. Include resources explaining Christian beliefs and details about your church. This equips Christians for spiritual discussions and serves as a visual reminder to share their faith.
- *Preach regularly on evangelism themes.* One organization taught its church planters to include five or six evangelism-themed sermons a year to keep the focus on outreach.[7] For those of us who preach: we should preach regularly on salvation, how to share our faith, or the church's role in evangelism. Keep the message encouraging—aiming for commitment, not guilt or anxiety. Regular preaching on evangelism helps make it a church-wide priority.

Evangelism will not become part of church culture if it is only mentioned occasionally. Regular reminders, training, and opportunities make it part of who we are, not just something we do sporadically. Take steps to keep the evangelistic temperature high—it will build a stronger, outreach-focused church.

The Importance of Church Leadership in Church Culture

These six principles will help us build evangelistic church cultures! But here is one more important piece of advice: building an evangelistic church culture starts with leadership. While leadership is not the only factor in a church's culture, it is usually the most influential one. Why is leadership so essential for an evangelistic church culture?

Leadership sets the tone. The way elders and ministers speak from the pulpit significantly shapes church culture. When they model love, spiritual depth, and an outreach mindset, it encourages the congregation to do the same.

Leadership example is key. To create a welcoming church, elders, ministers, and active members must take the lead in greeting visitors, building relationships, and following up. To create consistent outreach, leadership should organize and participate in church-wide inviting events, service projects, and visitor follow-ups. When leaders set the pace, others will follow.

Leadership points the way. Most Christians believe in evangelism but often need guidance on how to put it into action. Church leaders can provide direction by equipping and encouraging members, even if they are still learning how to navigate an ever-changing culture themselves.

In Judges 5:2, after Deborah and Barak's victory, they sing:

> *"That the leaders led in Israel,*
> *That the people volunteered,*
> *Bless the Lord!*

Notice it: the leaders led, and the people volunteered. Bless the Lord, indeed. That is how spiritual victories usually happen for God's people! To build an evangelistic culture, church leaders must lead through planning and example. As the congregation joins in, God will give the increase.

Start Building a Culture of Evangelism!

For effective evangelism in our culture, we need *church cultures that actively promote and support evangelism.* Individual efforts matter, but without healthy, salvation-focused church families, evangelism will struggle. Our post-Christian culture especially needs to see God's goodness reflected in a loving church family—one that cares for people and helps each other follow Christ. When churches embrace evangelism, it multiplies the gospel's impact.

In this chapter and the last, we have explored six key qualities for building an evangelistic church culture:

1) Loving People
2) Faith Commitment
3) Inviting and Hospitality
4) Doing Good to All People
5) Team Evangelism
6) Keeping the Evangelistic Temperature High

Be patient with your congregation—it takes time to build these qualities, and no church will do them perfectly. But step by step, as we cultivate these traits, a spirit of evangelism will grow in our church families. With God's help, let us commit to building evangelistic church cultures!

Discussion Questions

1) Were Jesus and his followers known for doing good to others? What examples can you give?
2) Should Christians only do good for one another, or should they do good for non-Christians as well? How does Galatians 6:10 help answer that question?
3) How does doing good for others help build an evangelistic church culture?

4) Is it okay for the church to serve others even if we do not share the gospel as we serve them? Did Jesus ever heal people and wait until later to talk with them about spiritual things? What can we learn from Jesus' example? Does that mean we should never share the gospel while serving others?

5) What are some ways your church family can start building a culture of doing good?

6) How does a culture of "team evangelism" encourage individual Christians to take part in evangelism?

7) What does "evangelistic temperature" mean? How can we keep an appropriately high evangelistic temperature in our church family?

8) What are some ways to appropriately celebrate those who have been baptized or have taken steps of faith? What does that type of celebration do for our church culture?

9) Do you agree that church leadership is essential in building an evangelistic church culture? What can church leaders do to lead the way?

10) Can you name the six culture qualities we have discussed in Chapters Ten and Eleven? Do you agree these six would build an evangelistic church culture? Which one seems like a great "next step" for your church family?

Personal Reflection

1) Do I show a Christian example of "doing good" in my own life? What can I do to serve others more in my life?

2) Do I personally encourage those who become Christians or take steps of faith? What can I do to encourage them more?

3) Is my personal "evangelistic temperature" high or low right now? How can I be more evangelism-conscious?

_____

Endnotes for Chapter 11

[1] One resource that highlights this characteristic of the early church:

Michael Frost, *Surprise the World: The Five Habits of Highly Missional People* (Colorado Springs, CO: Navpress, 2016), 7-10.

[2] Rick Richardson, *You Found Me: New Research on How Unchurched Nones, Millennials, and Irreligious Are Surprisingly Open to Christian Faith* (Downers Grove, IL: IVP Books, 2019), 170f.

[3] David M. Gustafson, *Gospel Witness: Evangelism in Word and Deed* (Grand Rapids, MI: Eerdmans, 2019), 106.

[4] If you have not read the book *When Helping Hurts*, it is worth reading as you process how best to help people:

Steve Corbett and Brian Fikkert, *When Helping Hurts: How to Alleviate Poverty Without Hurting the Poor...And Yourself*, expanded edition (Chicago, IL: Moody Publishers, 2012).

[5] For example, the writings of Kevin Harney:

Kevin Harney, *Organic Outreach for Ordinary People: Sharing Good News Naturally*, updated and expanded ed. (Grand Rapids, MI: Zondervan, 2018).

Kevin Harney, *Organic Outreach for Churches: Infusing Evangelistic Passion Into Your Congregation* (Grand Rapids, MI: Zondervan, 2011).

[6] G.L. Hawkins and Cally Parkinson, *Reveal: Where Are You?* (Barrington, IL: Willow Creek Resources, 2007), 45.

[7] Stan Granberg, who was leading the Kairos Church Planting Organization, in a class entitled *21st Century Evangelism* at Harding School of Theology, Spring semester 2011.

Chapter 12

Effective Evangelism
in Post-Christian Culture:

How to Study the Bible with Someone

"Philip ran up and heard him reading Isaiah the prophet, and said, 'Do you understand what you are reading?' And he said, 'Well, how could I, unless someone guides me?' And he invited Philip to come up and sit with him.

...

Then Philip opened his mouth, and beginning from this Scripture he preached Jesus to him." —Acts 8:30-31, 35

How Do I Study the Bible with Someone?

There are many ways to participate in the church's evangelistic mission, as we have seen throughout this book. But whenever we study evangelism, people often want to hear more about this question: "How do I study the Bible with someone?" Christians recognize that personal Bible studies play a crucial role in guiding people to Christ, yet many feel uncertain in this area. It is true, as we become more confident and better equipped to engage in Bible studies, our evangelism effectiveness will increase. And while learning to have personal Bible studies is important in every cultural context, even here there are some post-Christian principles to keep in mind.

In this chapter, we focus on this important topic by discussing the value of personal Bible studies, how they begin, key topics to cover, and practical advice for making them effective.

The Value of Personal Bible Studies

Why are personal Bible studies so important? First, they keep the spiritual conversation going, allowing growth to continue. When a non-Christian shows interest in Christianity, we want to nurture that curiosity. However, even with an issue as important as faith, life's distractions can quickly push it to the background. A regular Bible study together—perhaps weekly or biweekly—creates a rhythm of engagement, keeping God's word fresh in their minds and giving their faith the attention it needs to develop over time.

Second, personal Bible studies are valuable because people cannot become Christians unless someone shares the gospel with them. This is why many believers are eager to learn how to lead Bible studies effectively. While all aspects of the evangelistic process—spiritual conversations, invitations to church events, building relationships, and prayer—are vital, at some point, we must open the Bible and walk through the gospel together. A personal Bible study provides the space to do just that, helping our non-Christian friends understand Christianity in a deeper, more meaningful way and encouraging them toward faith in Christ.

Third, personal Bible studies offer the opportunity for individualized discussions about following Jesus. When an unbeliever visits a worship service or a Bible class, they hear the gospel, but in a larger group setting. While these experiences are valuable, many people need a more personal conversation to understand how the gospel applies to their specific life circumstances. That is the beauty of a *personal* Bible study—it allows seekers to ask questions, express doubts, and work through the barriers that may be holding them back. By meeting them where they are spiritually and guiding them forward in a focused, tailored way, we create an environment where faith can truly take root and grow.

How Personal Bible Studies Begin

So how do personal Bible studies start? At its core, it is simple: *someone must ask, and both parties must agree to meet and study together.* If those things do not happen, there will not be a Bible study. Since we can only control our part of that equation, it is worth considering how we can best extend the invitation.

Public Invitations Through Church Ministries

One way to encourage Bible studies is by offering them publicly through our congregational ministries. When people hear that Bible studies are available, some will take us up on the offer. There are several ways to share that invitation:

- Church Announcements: Regularly announcing the availability of Bible studies—especially during visitor-friendly events like a Friends and Family Sunday—can help seekers consider the opportunity to explore faith more deeply. Even if no one responds, these announcements remind members, including young and growing Christians, that their church values evangelistic Bible studies (which keeps the evangelistic temperature up).
- Community Outreach Materials: If your church sends newsletters or bulletins to the community, including an offer for personal Bible studies ensures that even those who are not attending services know the opportunity exists.
- Church Website and Social Media: A dedicated page on your church's website explaining how Bible studies work, along with a contact form, makes it easy for people to sign up. Periodically sharing this information on the church's social media can further extend the invitation.

By publicly making it clear that personal Bible studies are valuable and available, we create more opportunities for people to request a study.

Personal Invitations from Christians

While public invitations are helpful, the most common way Bible studies begin is through a personal invitation from a Christian. It is rare for a non-Christian to initiate a study on their own—most of the time, we must take the first step.

Knowing when to ask requires wisdom. If we are having a spiritual conversation with someone who seems interested in Christianity, we might decide the next step is to say, "Would you be interested in getting together to talk more about this?" Or if a non-Christian has been visiting church for a while, someone should be ready to engage them in faith conversations and, when the time feels right, offer a Bible study. The key is to be attentive and prayerful, always looking for opportunities to extend the invitation.

Overcoming the Fear of Rejection

Evangelism—like anything in life—comes with the possibility of rejection. If someone declines a Bible study, that is okay. We can simply say, "No problem; just remember the offer is open if you ever want to talk more." Then, continue being a kind and supportive Christian friend, keeping them in our prayers. We must not let fear of rejection prevent us from offering a study when the moment seems right.

One of my ministry friends who spent years in foreign missions calls this moment "The Big Ask." He believes in the power of personal Bible studies and consistently seeks opportunities to invite people to be part of them. Yet, even after making the invitation countless times, he admits that he still feels a little nervous before asking. His advice: take a deep breath (at least mentally) and just ask. If they say yes, set a time and place, exchange contact information, and let them know you are looking forward to it. If they say no, let them know the invitation stands, then continue being a supportive friend.

For most people on their journey to faith, a Christian—whether a minister, parent, friend, or church member—will need to extend a personal invitation to study the Bible. Every church needs members who are ready and willing to offer personal Bible studies, helping others move closer to Christ.

What Do We Study? Choosing Topics for Personal Bible Studies

One of the key principles in this chapter is understanding that *personal Bible studies can take two different forms*:

1) *Teacher-Led Studies* – In this format, one person takes the lead as the teacher, guiding the study and helping the other person learn more about Christianity.

2) *Discussion-Based Studies* – In this format, everyone involved— whether two, three, or more people—engages in open discussion, without the expectation that anyone is the primary teacher.

If we believe a personal Bible study is the next step for someone, we must use wisdom to determine which type of study best suits their situation. The choice depends on the individual's level of interest and what they are looking for in a study. If they seem eager to learn about faith *from us*, a teacher-led study will be the best approach. If they are more interested in ongoing faith conversations *with us*, a discussion-based study will feel more natural and appropriate.

Both study types are valuable—the goal is to keep the faith conversation going. However, recognizing the distinction is important. If someone is not expecting a formal teacher-student dynamic, assuming that role may make them uncomfortable. On the other hand, if they are seeking clear guidance on faith, a structured, teacher-led study may be exactly what they need.

We will consider both types of studies, when each might be appropriate, and what kind of material works best for each approach.

Teacher-Led Studies: Studies Where You Take the Lead

A teacher-led study is most effective when someone has expressed interest in Christianity and wants to learn more. For example:

- A non-Christian friend has asked about your faith and seems open to exploring Christianity.
- Someone who has visited your church has specific questions about what your congregation believes.

In these cases, offering a Bible study is a natural next step. You might say something like: *"I would love for us to get together and talk more. We could study what the Bible teaches and let you explore it for yourself. Would you be interested in that?"* If they are open to learning, they will likely appreciate this kind of structured study.

In a teacher-led format, what should you study? If they have specific questions, start there. Research the topic beforehand so you can provide a well-prepared, thoughtful response. However, if they want a basic understanding of Christianity, a structured study covering six key topics is often helpful:

1. Scripture – The structure of the Bible, its overarching message, and how Christians view it as God's inspired word.

2. Jesus – His identity, teachings, miracles, death, resurrection, and promised return.

3. Sin and the Cross – How sin separates us from God and how Jesus' sacrifice restores that relationship.

4. How to Become a Christian – Faith, repentance, and baptism in the teachings of Jesus and the apostles, including examples from the book of Acts showing how we receive salvation through Christ.

5. <u>The Church</u> – God's design for the church, its purpose, and its role in a Christian's life.

6. <u>Spiritual Growth</u> – The importance of staying faithful, growing in Christ, and living out one's faith.

Each of these topics will take at least one study session, perhaps longer depending on the discussion. You might also encourage "homework" between meetings, such as reading through the gospel of Matthew or Acts. Homework readings foster continued growth in between meetings and allow your friend to engage with Scripture on their own.

If you are not comfortable leading studies without structured materials, there are many excellent Bible study guides available. It is a good idea to find one you trust and have it ready, so you are prepared when an opportunity arises. Churches can also keep these resources on hand for members to use. Knowing what material you would study with a non-Christian is an important step toward feeling equipped for sharing the gospel.

Discussion-Based Studies: Studies Where No One is the "Teacher"

In some cases, a formal teacher-student structure is not the best fit. For example:

- You have a friend with a different religious background or different beliefs, and every now and then you have conversations about the differences.

- You have a neighbor who likes to talk about religion and considers himself a Christian, but you can see that his life and faith practices do not line up with Scripture.

In these cases, your friend might not feel the need for instruction *from* you, but they enjoy discussing the Bible *with* you. That is a great opportunity!

This is especially common in today's post-Christian religious landscape, where many people have heard bits and pieces of Christianity but have never studied the Bible for themselves. Instead of offering to "teach" them, you can suggest simply reading and discussing Scripture together. For example, you might say: *"Would you like to start meeting up to read and talk about the Bible together? Maybe we could go through the gospel of Matthew a chapter or two at a time."*

In a discussion-based study, reading through one of the gospels would be a great way to start. You could read one or two chapters each week, either together or as homework. When you meet, you can discuss questions such as: (1) What stands out to you in these chapters? (2) What questions do these passages raise? (3) How can we apply these teachings to our lives?

Be sure to connect the study to real-life application, showing how Scripture shapes how we live. Also, pray together at the end of each meeting, about the Scripture you studied and about your lives, asking God to guide both of you in your faith journey. Then decide what chapters you will read for next time and set a time to meet again.

This format allows faith conversations to continue naturally. Over time, different spiritual issues will come up, giving opportunity to take detours and discuss those questions more deeply. For example, if you were studying through Matthew, Jesus being baptized in Matthew chapter 3 allows a study on what the Bible says about baptism. The Sermon on the Mount (Matthew 5-7) brings up many challenging teachings on how to live as a follower of Christ. Jesus' teachings on tradition (Matthew 15) and the church (Matthew 16) could open conversations about denominational traditions versus biblical teachings. Whatever detours are or are not taken, as the conversation continues over time, God can use his word to change hearts and lives.

Personal Bible studies with people are powerful, even if they do not begin with us "teaching them." If we can engage in discussion-based studies that keep the conversation going, it will deepen the relationship and faith will grow. As you engage in the study, keep in mind those "spiritual conversation principles" from Chapters Eight and Nine, patiently looking to encourage the next steps at the right times.

Both study formats—teacher-led and discussion-based—serve the important purpose of bringing people into closer contact with God's word. The more comfortable we become with both, the more opportunities we will have to share the gospel and help others grow in their faith. And as we teach and study with others, we will find ourselves growing as well.

Practical Advice for Personal Bible Studies

Whether you are new to personal Bible studies or have led many before, these tips can help make our study time more meaningful. Several of these reiterate post-Christian evangelism principles from earlier chapters:

Building Connection and Trust

- Start and end with real-life conversations. Begin with a simple, "How has your week been?" and end with, "Before we go, what can we pray about together?" Build a sense of being on each other's team. Genuine relationships are an important foundation for effective Bible studies.
- Show that your faith brings joy and purpose, even when life is difficult. Let them see how Christianity makes a real, positive difference in your life.
- Be authentic about your own journey. Acknowledge that you are not perfect, and that faith is a continuous process of growth.

Focus on Scripture, Not Opinions

- Let the Bible speak. Read directly from Scripture and emphasize that you are simply seeking to understand and apply God's word, not personal opinions. It is God's Spirit-inspired word that convicts hearts and brings transformation.

- Avoid debates that distract from Scripture. If a conversation starts leaning too much on personal opinions, gently guide it back to what the Bible says.

Maintaining Respect and Humility

- Handle disagreements with kindness. If you do not agree on something, respond with patience and a Christ-like spirit. As one writer says it, "Never win the point and lose the person."[1]
- Never come across as arrogant or superior. We are all sinners in need of grace, and our goal is to humbly help others find salvation in Jesus.
- Be wise regarding one-on-one male-female Bible studies. To avoid any appearance of impropriety, consider having another Christian present.

Navigating Questions and Next Steps

- It is okay not to have all the answers. If you do not know how to answer a question, say, "That is a great question! Let me study that more, and we can talk about it next time." This shows humility and keeps the conversation going for another meeting.
- Never apologize for biblical truth—but always share it with love. Stand by God's word and deliver it with kindness and respect.
- Encourage, but do not pressure. People need time to process life decisions. Especially in our post-Christian culture, people do not respond well to "hard selling," whether in business or in faith. A simple invitation—to a worship service, a church event, or to be baptized into Christ—can be powerful, but give them space to make the decision themselves.
- As the person seems ready to become a Christian, encourage them and let them know you would love to see them take that step, but give them enough space to make sure it is their own

commitment and choice. When it happens, celebrate with them.

Be Patient and Trust God

- Patience is important. Many people in today's culture need space to learn, ask questions, and reflect before making a commitment to Christ. Spiritual growth takes time.

- If you feel interest has waned or they seem stuck, it is okay to take a break from the studies. God will keep working in their life. Stay in contact as a friend, and maybe after a few months, see if they would like to resume studying together.

- Trust God to use your efforts. You will not always say the perfect thing, and that is okay. Pray for God's guidance in what you say and for his work in the life of the person with whom you are studying (Col. 4:2-4). Do your best. Learn as you go. God can use even our imperfect conversations and studies to draw souls closer to him.

Personal Bible studies should be focused on God's word, but they are not just about sharing knowledge—they are also about walking alongside someone as they grow in faith. Approach each study with love, patience, and prayer, and trust God to do the transforming work.

An Important Part of God's Evangelistic Mission

The more Christians become better equipped to engage in *personal Bible studies*, the more evangelism opportunities will increase. Personal Bible studies are not the only way to participate in God's evangelistic mission, but they are an important step for most people to come to Christ. Imagine the impact if just 10% of your church family started having personal Bible studies with people in their lives —even if they all began as simple, discussion-based studies of reading the Bible together. What if that number grew to 25% or even 50%? Just think of how God could use those many studies to convict hearts with his word! The more we study the Bible with others, the more faith will grow.

At the very least, every church family needs members who are ready and willing to study the Bible with non-Christians who visit. Ministers, church leaders, and mature Christians should take the lead in this effort, like other areas of church evangelism. Churches can also equip members through training and Bible classes focused on the practical aspects of personal Bible studies.

If you desire to grow in being part of personal Bible studies, that is great! Like anything else, you will learn as you go. A good way to start is by asking someone in your church family—perhaps a minister—if you could sit in on a Bible study to observe and learn. And as you grow in this area, remember you will never be perfect at it. Not everyone will say yes to a study, and not everyone will respond the way you hope. Sometimes you will have a Bible study and wish you had said something differently. (In fact, that will probably happen most of the time you have studies with people!) But that is how we grow in any area: we have successes and failures, we learn from them, and we develop wisdom. Through it all, God works in us, building our own faith and the faith of others also. Do your best to grow in this area, and God will use your efforts to bring souls closer to him.

Discussion Questions

1) Have you ever been part of a personal Bible study? How did it begin? What do you remember about it?
2) Why are personal Bible studies important for helping people come to Christ?
3) How do personal Bible studies begin?
4) How can churches offer personal Bible studies in a public way?
5) Do you agree that Christians usually need to ask the non-Christian if they want to be part of a Bible study, instead of waiting for them to ask us? Why?

6) How should we handle it if someone says no to our offer of a personal Bible study?

7) Do you agree there are two different types of personal Bible studies? Why might it be important to recognize what type of study the other person wants?

8) If someone wants to learn about Christianity from us (a teacher-led study), what topics should we study with them in personal Bible studies? Do you think those could be covered in just one time studying together, or will it be a longer process?

9) If you and a friend begin a personal Bible study in which no one is taking the lead as the "teacher" (a discussion-based study), what could you study together?

10) Do you agree that simply reading through a book of the Bible with someone in a regular Bible study can lead to opportunities to discuss serious matters of faith with them? How might that happen?

Personal Reflection

1) When I was thinking about becoming a Christian, did someone have a personal Bible study with me? How did that work? Have I been part of a personal Bible study since I became a Christian? What can I learn from those Bible study experiences?

2) Imagine asking someone to be part of a personal Bible study. How would I say it in my own personality? First, how might I ask if someone is not a Christian and seems interested in learning more about my faith? Second, how might I ask if I have a friend who is open to talking about spiritual things, but may not be ready for me to "teach" them?

3) How can I begin growing in my ability to have personal Bible studies with people? Is there someone in my church family I could ask to join next time they lead a personal Bible study?

Endnotes for Chapter 12

[1] Gary S. Comer, *Soul Whisperer: Why the Church Must Change the Way It Views Evangelism* (Eugene, OR: Resource Publications, 2013), 173.

SECTION THREE:
Conclusion and Next Steps

Chapter 13

Chapter 13

Conclusion and Next Steps:

Thinking Bigger About What is Possible

"Now to Him who is able to do far more abundantly beyond all that we ask or think, according to the power that works within us, to Him be the glory in the church and in Christ Jesus to all generations forever and ever. Amen." —Ephesians 3:20-21

What Now?

Over the last twelve chapters, as promised, we have taken consistent themes and best practices from recent evangelism studies and brought them together into a set of post-Christian evangelism principles. These are principles that Christians have found effective for evangelism in our changing cultural context, and they help us answer the question so many Christians have been asking in the last few decades: how do you share the gospel in our culture?

Some of these principles are *biblical mindset shifts*, such as being patient, understanding it will often take time for people to learn and process the gospel message. Some of these principles are *biblical qualities to develop*, such as seeking wisdom in how and when we discuss faith with others.

Some of these principles are *biblical habits to build*, such as evangelistic prayer, having spiritual conversations, and encouraging the next step.

Here is an overview of the post-Christian evangelism principles we have seen in this study:

1) *Evangelism Perspective*—Understanding the cultural landscape, both its challenges and its opportunities. Maintaining a positive outlook on evangelism. Recommitting ourselves to evangelism and learning to "think like missionaries" in how we share the gospel in our changing culture. (Chapters One and Two)

2) *Evangelistic Prayer*—Praying regularly for souls and open doors for the gospel, and trusting God to provide evangelistic opportunities, relationships, and timing. (Chapter Three)

3) *Evangelistic Patience*—Recognizing that most people in our culture start further away spiritually than previous generations, we must learn to be patient with a longer process of non-Christians coming to Christ. (Chapter Four)

4) *Evangelism Personalities*—Realizing not every Christian will be evangelists in the mold of Paul or Peter. We each contribute to the church's evangelistic mission in different ways, just like Christians did in the New Testament. (Chapter Five)

5) *Evangelistic Motives*—Being authentic in our love for people, avoiding ulterior motives or manipulation. Rejecting anxiety-driven or self-centered motivations and embracing healthier motives for evangelism and relationships. (Chapter Six)

6) *Evangelism Pathways: Building Relationships*—Recognizing that most people come to Christ through relationships. Encouraging Christians to cultivate authentic relationships with people in their lives who are not yet Christians. (Chapter Seven)

7) *Evangelism and Faith Conversations*—Understanding that post-Christian culture is not always open to sermons or memorized presentations but is open to conversations and genuine dialogue. Learning how to have meaningful faith conversations. (Chapters Eight and Nine)

8) *Evangelistic Church Cultures*—Realizing there are limitations to "lone ranger" evangelism if we do not have a healthy church family alongside us. The need to build evangelistic church cultures, which provide a multiplying effect for evangelistic encouragement. (Chapters Ten and Eleven)

9) *Evangelistic Bible Studies*—A bonus chapter on how to study the Bible with people, including the need to recognize some post-Christian dynamics in those studies. The need for every church to have Christians who are willing and able to lead personal Bible studies. (Chapter Twelve)

That is quite a list of valuable concepts! I hope you have found these principles to be biblical, and I hope you have found them to be helpful. As we bring the study toward a close, the natural question is "What now?" The goal of these discussions is not just to read about the best concepts in post-Christian evangelism; the goal is to apply these things so we can help unbelievers draw closer to Christ.

In this final chapter, we will summarize our next steps under the idea of "thinking bigger" about evangelism. It will serve as a good one-last-look at what we have studied, and it will highlight some first steps down the path toward more-effective evangelism. Now that we are all better equipped for post-Christian evangelism, how can we *think bigger* going forward?

Thinking Bigger...About What Is Most Important

Sometimes we forget what is most important in life. As Jesus explains the Christian commitment in Matthew 16:24-26, he reminds us that our souls are the most important thing:

Then Jesus said to His disciples, "If anyone wishes to come after Me, he must deny himself, and take up his cross and follow Me.

...

For what will it profit a man if he gains the whole world and forfeits his soul? Or what will a man give in exchange for his soul?"

The entire message of Scripture reminds us that God cares deeply about saving souls. Throughout the Bible, God reaches out to sinful humanity, offering salvation in life and eternity through relationship with him. As Jesus celebrated the salvation of Zaccheus, he summarized his own life mission: *"The Son of Man has come to seek and to save that which was lost"* (Luke 19:10). When the Pharisees criticized Jesus for spending time with sinners, he told three parables to explain that God seeks lost souls, and that heaven celebrates every time a soul comes back to God (Luke 15:1-32). The Bible makes it clear: God cares deeply about souls coming back to him.

We are all busy. Too busy. One of life's constant challenges is to keep perspective on what is most important, and to make decisions about what is worth our time. Having studied evangelism in our culture, we need to "think bigger" about how we use our time. Of course, we need to put time into work and family and other life commitments, and it is also important to enjoy our God-given blessings (1 Tim. 6:17). But may we also build evangelistic practices into our regular life rhythms. Will we make time to pray daily for souls in our life? Will we make time to build relationships, over coffee or lunch or inviting people into our homes? Will we make the effort to greet visitors at our church assemblies and activities? Will we make time to study the Bible with people when the opportunities arise? All these things will require time and energy, but in God's eyes, those sacrifices are more than worth it.

It is not enough to *know* how to produce effective evangelism; we must *live it out*. True alignment with God's heart comes when we put evangelistic principles into practice in our everyday lives. Let us *think bigger* about what truly matters in life and commit to building evangelistic practices into our regular life routines.

Thinking Bigger...Than the Challenges

Our current American culture presents challenges for sharing the gospel. Secularism has been on the rise, and Christianity is often met with skepticism or even disdain. Many people form opinions about Christianity before they have ever met a Christian, visited a church, or heard the teachings of Jesus firsthand. In a society where trust is scarce and cynicism runs deep, people often assume hidden agendas and doubt that anything— even something good—can be genuine.

It can be discouraging to see fewer Americans professing faith, to witness how many have drifted away from Christianity in recent decades, and to recognize how the constant noise of wealth, busyness, and entertainment can drown out people's awareness of their spiritual needs.[1]

So yes, the challenges are real. But we need to *think bigger* than the challenges. While it is important to understand our cultural context so we can engage it wisely, we must resist the temptation to let discouragement define our mindset. We do not reflect on these cultural shifts to give up; rather, we reflect so we can press forward with wisdom, intentionality, and faith. God's mission has not changed, and more importantly, neither has God.

Remember the promise Jesus gave after commissioning his disciples to take the gospel to all nations: *"I am with you always, even to the end of the age"* (Matt. 28:20). God is always with his people. The gospel is still "the power of God for salvation" (Rom. 1:16). It still transforms lives, just as it has transformed ours. Remember that God can turn cultures around—he did it many times in Scripture, and he has done it several times in our country's history as well. Remember that Christianity continues to grow globally and is projected to keep growing in the years to come.

Remember also that there are still open doors in our culture. While many Americans identify in surveys as having "no religion," most of those have not really rejected Christianity, and many of them still visit churches regularly.[2] The majority of unchurched Americans are willing to visit church events if invited by a Christian they know and trust, an open door we have noted several times in this study.[3] Many people in our country are still open to Christianity, if only we can create and grow the relationship pathways that lead to faith.[4]

Yes, there are challenges, but Christianity has flourished in difficult cultures before, and it can again. God is still present, the gospel is still powerful, and open doors are still before us.

Thinking Bigger...Than "It-All-Depends-on-Me Evangelism"

We want to be committed to evangelism without being anxious about it. Too often, believers fall into the trap of "it-all-depends-on-me" evangelism—feeling pressured to say everything perfectly, fearing that our mistakes might push someone further from faith. This mindset can lead to unnecessary guilt if someone has not responded to the gospel, or it can cause us to inappropriately pressure non-Christians. As a result, many Christians feel anxious and fearful about evangelism.

When we *think bigger* about God's evangelistic mission, we remember that the responsibility does not rest solely on our shoulders. Here are a few other evangelism factors to keep in mind:

- *God is already working in the world and in people's lives.* This is his mission, we are simply joining him in it. God prepares hearts long before we meet someone, and his work continues long after our interactions end. God leads the way, shaping lives, hearts, and cultures to best hear his word.
- *Each soul has the responsibility to seek God.* Scripture makes it clear that people must make their own decision about faith

(Rom. 1:19-21, Acts 17:27). Even when Jesus preached, some people chose not to follow. In the Parable of the Sower, the same seed—the word of God—falls on different types of hearts, some receptive and some resistant (Matt. 13:1-23). Our role is to faithfully share the message, but it is up to each person to decide how they will respond.

- *Evangelism is the mission of the church, not just me.* I am a small part of a much larger mission, one that requires all Christians serving in different roles to spread the gospel around the world. I can only do my part, and I am not alone.

- *My words and actions will never be perfect in evangelism.* It will never be my own perfect words that bring someone to salvation. It is God's word that convicts hearts and leads people to Christ. People are not combination locks that automatically open if the right words are spoken. Rather, each soul must make their own heart decision, and God will work even through our imperfect efforts to teach and encourage.

Let us be fully committed to God's mission, but without anxiety, fear, or the pressure of unrealistic expectations. Someone else's salvation does not depend solely on me. My responsibility is to be a faithful influence, share the truth with love, and trust that God is working through it all.

Thinking Bigger...About the Most Common Pathway to Christianity in Our Culture

How do people usually come to Christ in our post-Christian culture? In a culture that knows less about the Bible and true Christian teaching, conversions rarely happen after one conversation or sermon. While it does occur, most people need more time to learn, reflect, and process the decision to become a Christian. And in a culture that is often skeptical of strangers—especially when it comes to religion—mass media campaigns and door-knocking efforts, though they still produce good things, are not the primary ways people come to faith.

The most common pathway to Christianity in our culture is relationship-based, and it takes time. Most people begin their journey toward Christ because of a personal connection with a Christian—whether a family member, friend, coworker, or someone they encounter through life circumstances. Over time, these relationships open doors to meaningful spiritual conversations, which eventually lead to steps toward Christ.

Those steps vary from person to person, but they often include: accepting an invitation for their first visit to a church event; meeting other Christians who are encouraging and authentic; asking questions about Christianity and receiving patient, encouraging answers; becoming more involved in church activities; appreciating how a church family truly loves God and people; continued conversations about faith; participating in a Bible study to seriously consider Christianity; deciding to be baptized into Christ.

Of course, each person's journey is unique, and the steps toward Christ will not always follow a straight line. There may be times when their interest seems to wane or their church involvement becomes inconsistent. But in general, that is the most common path: personal relationships lead to spiritual conversations, which eventually produce steps toward Christ. It is relationship-based, and it takes time.

Understanding the most common pathway to Christianity helps us set appropriate expectations for evangelism. Instead of pushing too quickly, we can focus on building relationships with sincerity, valuing the friendship itself—whether or not they ever choose to become a Christian—and keeping our eyes open for opportunities to discuss faith. We can *think bigger* by embracing the process of encouraging people one step at a time, trusting that they will see the goodness of Christianity in our lives and in our church family, in hopes that they will eventually desire to follow God themselves.

Build genuine relationships, and patiently encourage people one step at a time.

Thinking Bigger...About My Own Next Steps

What practical steps can we take to be more evangelistic in our daily lives? Here are a few "next steps" we can integrate into our regular routines:

- *Make evangelistic prayer a daily habit.* Pray specifically for the people in your life who have not yet come to Christ. Ask God to open doors for the gospel. Pray for our culture to be more receptive to God's truth.
- *Be a blessing to the people God has placed in your life.* Build genuine relationships with both Christians and non-Christians. Enjoy getting to know people, showing interest in their lives. Get coffee or have someone over to eat. Show Christ-like love, especially when people are hurting.
- *Help cultivate an evangelistic church culture.* In your church family, help build a spirit of love and community. Greet visitors and get to know them. Be involved in serving others. Be committed to your church assemblies and opportunities.
- *Understand your own "evangelism personality" and embrace your role.* Reflect on how your unique gifts contribute to the broader mission of evangelism (see Chapter Five). Understand how you fit in the bigger picture and fill your role as best you can.
- *Have spiritual conversations when the opportunities arise.* When faith comes up in conversation, do not shy away from it. Ask thoughtful questions and listen well. Learn where people are spiritually and encourage the next step in their faith. (And practice the principles of Chapters Eight and Nine!)
- *Give invitations to church events.* Look for opportunities to invite a non-Christian friend or family member to a church event. When someone accepts your invitation, be there to

welcome them, introduce them to others, and help them feel comfortable.

- *Consider preparing for Bible study opportunities.* This step may not be for everyone, but every church needs members who are ready to engage in personal Bible studies. Whether teacher-led or discussion-based (see Chapter Twelve), Bible studies keep the faith conversation going and allow faith to deepen. Not every Christian will be a teacher (James 3:1), but if this fits your God-given personality and abilities, the church needs you to fill this role. Be prepared to guide someone through a multi-lesson introduction to Christianity when the opportunity arises.

Many Christians simply do not know how to evangelize in our culture, but having studied this topic, let us *think bigger* and make these practices part of our lives. Christians have found these practical steps to produce evangelistic opportunities, even in our post-Christian context. If we incorporate them into our life routines, we will see open doors for the gospel, in our life and in our church family. The gospel has always spread through individual Christians living out their faith and engaging their unique corners of the world with intentionality. Let us commit to taking these steps, trusting that God will work through them.

Thinking Bigger...About Our Church Family's Next Steps

One of the most important goals from this study is to build an evangelistic church culture—where evangelism is not just an occasional effort but a defining characteristic of who we are as a church family. As we discussed in Chapters Ten and Eleven, here are some key qualities we want to cultivate in our congregation:

1) A Culture of Loving People
2) A Culture of Faith Commitment
3) A Culture of Inviting and Hospitality
4) A Culture of Doing Good to All People

5) A Culture of Team Evangelism

6) A Culture That Keeps the Evangelistic Temperature High

Here are a few practical steps to help churches get started:

1) *Strengthen the church's health first.* It may be wise to start by reinforcing a culture of love, unity, and togetherness before focusing on outreach. This is especially true if your congregation has recently faced challenges (as many churches do from time to time). Once those unifying qualities are better-established, outreach will be easier and more effective.

2) *Engage church leaders in the conversation.* While every member plays a role, church leaders—elders, ministers, and other key figures—set the tone for building an evangelistic culture. Some of these qualities do not require formal leadership goals—for example, every Christian should help build a culture of loving people—but building an evangelistic church culture happens best when the church leaders understand what they want to build and lead by example.

3) *Be patient and think long term.* Cultures are not built overnight; they take time. It is usually unwise to push too much too fast. Think long-term, and piece by piece, you will see these qualities grow in your church family.

4) *Give grace and keep moving forward.* Remember that your church family will never do these things perfectly. Do not let that discourage you. Give yourselves grace and commit to continuous improvement. Encourage one another and celebrate progress along the way.

Evangelistic church cultures are important for post-Christian evangelism! *Think bigger* about what your church family can be, and with God's help, create an environment that truly encourages souls to draw closer to God. When evangelism is woven into the very identity of a congregation, the church becomes a beacon of faith, hope, and love in the community.

Thinking Bigger...About the Possibilities

Evangelism in post-Christian culture is usually a slower process.[5] As we described the most common pathway to Christ above: it is relationship-based, and it takes time. It takes time to build relationships. It takes time for people to learn and process real Christianity. It takes time for people to take the life steps that lead to Christ. And then after people become Christians, it takes time to keep walking with them as they grow.

With a slower process, how can we increase effective evangelism? We need more evangelism-minded Christians! Since it takes time for people to come to Christ, we need more Christians involved in the process. No believer can build relationships with everyone, so we need lots of Christians building relationships. Each Christian will have unique opportunities for the gospel, opportunities no one else will have. Imagine the impact if every Christian took the evangelistic steps we listed in this chapter!

We also need more evangelistic church cultures. Every church family has unique opportunities to reach people, opportunities for the gospel that no other congregation will have. Imagine the impact if every church became known for its love, faith commitment, hospitality, service, teamwork, and enthusiasm for evangelism—we need more evangelistic church families!

If Christians and churches recommit themselves to evangelism, there are many reasons to be hopeful about the future. In fact, some wonder if our culture is beginning a pendulum swing back toward faith.[6] Pew Research Center found that 62% of American adults identified as Christians in 2024, which is far less than fifty years ago, but is a slight uptick from a low point of 60% in 2022.[7] That could be mere statistical variance, or it could suggest a shift toward Christianity. Barna's latest research has shown even more confidence that our culture is becoming more open to Christianity, declaring there has been a "groundswell of commitment to Jesus over the last four years."[8] Their 2025 study found that 66% of all U.S. adults say they have made a personal commitment to Jesus that is still important in their life today, a 12-percentage-point increase since 2021, spearheaded by increased faith in the younger adult generations, Millennials and Gen Z. Anecdotally, I have noticed more people reacting against secular values and turning to God or renewing their faith in Christ. We also see evangelism potential in Americans' abiding belief in God: we are still a country in which 83% of adults say they believe in God or a higher power,[9] an open door for encouraging people toward Christ. Moreover, thanks to the extensive reflection on culture and evangelism over the past few decades, Christians are "catching up" to our culture's criticisms and challenges, learning to navigate them more faithfully and effectively.[10] More Christians and churches are recognizing how our culture has changed, finding their footing, and successfully moving forward. Yes, there are still many challenges, and we do not know the future; but in general, you can count me among the optimists.

Of course, the greatest reason for optimism is the unwavering presence of God, who remains bigger than any challenge. Jesus began his ministry with twelve disciples, and God used them to change the world. Surely there are more than twelve of us who will recommit to living evangelistically. Who knows, perhaps God will use our renewed dedication as a spark not only to bring souls back to him, but maybe to help shift our entire culture back toward him.

With the same God and the same gospel working in us, there are no limits to what God can do. That is what the apostle Paul reminds us about God in Ephesians 3:20-21:

Now to Him who is able to do far more abundantly beyond all that
we ask or think, according to the power that works within us, to

Him be the glory in the church and in Christ Jesus to all generations forever and ever. Amen.

Walking with God, we need to *think bigger* about what is possible. It is time to get started! Having studied post-Christian evangelism, we are better equipped than ever before. Let us build evangelistic practices into our life rhythms and equip other Christians to do the same. Let us build evangelistic qualities into the fabric of our church family and encourage other church families to do the same. I will be giving it my best effort and I trust you will also. Let us shine God's light as best we can in our post-Christian culture, trusting God to give the increase, and all to his glory.

Discussion Questions

1) What do you think is the biggest challenge to sharing the gospel in our post-Christian culture?

2) In this study on post-Christian evangelism, are there any specific concepts or principles you have found especially helpful? What principles do you wish other Christians could hear?

3) Do the principles we have studied resonate with your experience? Do you agree that these steps will produce effective evangelism in our culture?

4) Do we struggle to keep evangelistic practices in our life routines? Why? How can we do better?

5) Do you agree that the most common pathway to Christianity in our culture is relationship-based and takes time? Have you seen that process in your life or in someone from your church family? Is that the only pathway to Christianity in our culture?

6) What are some specific "next steps" for individual Christians to apply this study in their lives?

7) What are some specific "next steps" for churches to apply this study in their church families?

8) Are there any reasons to be hopeful about evangelism effectiveness in our culture?

Personal Reflection

1) Is my life an example of genuine Christian faith? What do I need to do better in my life, so that people will see a genuine (not perfect, but genuine) Christian life in me?

2) How can I take the individual "next steps" listed in this chapter, making evangelistic activities a bigger part of my life? How can I make these things part of my regular life routines? (Remember, it is not enough for us just to know these things, we actually have to do them!)

3) Am I ready to be committed to God's evangelistic mission? What is holding me back? Let me start by committing myself to prayer, for God to use my life to help spread the gospel!

Endnotes for Chapter 13

[1] Barna Group, *Reviving Evangelism: Current Realities that Demand a New Vision for Sharing Faith* (Ventura, CA: Barna Group, 2019), 12, 19.

[2] Ryan Burge, interview with CT Magazine entitled "Most 'Nones' Still Keep the Faith" (CT Magazine, February 24, 2021). Burge's studies found that 2/3 of "nones" still go to church at least once a year, remaining connected with Christians.

Also: Jim Davis, Michael Graham, Ryan P. Burge. *The Great Dechurching: Who's Leaving, Why Are They Going, and What Will It Take to Bring Them Back?* (Grand Rapids, MI: Zondervan, 2023), 27-29.

Also: Rick Richardson, *You Found Me: New Research on How Unchurched Nones, Millennials, and Irreligious Are Surprisingly Open to Christian Faith* (Downers Grove, IL: IVP Books, 2019).

[3] Thom S. Rainer, *The Unchurched Next Door* (Grand Rapids, MI: Zondervan, 2003), 232.

Also: Rick Richardson, *You Found Me: New Research on How Unchurched Nones, Millennials, and Irreligious Are Surprisingly Open to Christian Faith* (Downers Grove, IL: IVP Books, 2019), 61f.

[4] Several studies note that personal relationships are the most common pathway to the Christian faith. (These are listed in the Chapter Seven endnotes also.)

- Shawn D. Anderson, *Living Dangerously*. A nationwide survey found that 70% of Christians said there was a key individual who was influential in leading them to Christ. (Eugene, OR: Wipf and Stock, 2010), 28.

- Gary S. Comer, *Soul Whisperer: Why the Church Must Change the Way It Views Evangelism*. Points to a New England study of recent Christian converts, in which 71% said a relationship with a caring Christian friend was the most important factor (Eugene, OR: Resource Publications, 2013), 141. (Also see footnote on p. 141.)

- Barna Group, *Translating the Great Commission: What Spreading the Gospel Means to U.S. Christians in the 21st Century*. A 2018 Barna Research study of U.S. churchgoers (not just new converts) found that 19% became Christians through conversations with a Christian they knew personally, and many more (48%) as a result of relationships with their Christian family members. (Ventura, CA: The Barna Group, 2018), 22-23.

- Michael Green, *Evangelism in the Early Church*, rev. ed. England— another post-Christian culture—shows similar results: Green appeals to British surveys revealing that most new Christians regard a close relationship with a Christian as the most important factor in their conversion (Grand Rapids, MI: Eerdmans, 2003), 24.

[5] See Chapter Four for more on this. For examples, notice in these two sources below the summary charts about how post-Christian evangelism is different from evangelism in past American generations. There is a consistent emphasis on a longer process:

Will McRaney, Jr. *The Art of Personal Evangelism: Sharing Jesus in a Changing Culture* (Nashville, TN: Broadman and Holman, 2003), 165.

John P. Bowen, *Evangelism for "Normal" People: Good News for Those Looking for a Fresh Approach* (Minneapolis, MN: Augsburg Fortress, 2002), 147.

[6] For example: "Is Christianity in America Back? Five Key Findings from Landmark Survey." *Newsweek* online article, February 28, 2025. Accessed May 6, 2025 at https://www.newsweek.com/christianity-back-america-pew-research-poll-key-findings-2037493.

[7] Pew Research Center 2024 Survey, released February 26, 2025. Accessed on May 6, 2025 at: https://www.pewresearch.org/religion/2025/02/26/decline-of-christianity-in-the-us-has-slowed-may-have-leveled-off/

[8] Barna, "New Research: Belief in Jesus Rises, Fueled by Young Adults." Online article, April 7, 2025. Accessed May 6, 2025 at https://www.barna.com/research/belief-in-jesus-rises/

[9] Pew Research Center 2024 Survey, released February 26, 2025. Accessed on May 6, 2025 at: https://www.pewresearch.org/religion/2025/02/26/decline-of-christianity-in-the-us-has-slowed-may-have-leveled-off/

[10] Many good resources have helped Christians understand how to address some of our secular culture's most common criticisms, and appropriate responses are becoming better known in our religious world. Helpful resources include works such as:

Timothy Keller, *The Reason for God: Belief in an Age of Skepticism* (New York: Riverhead Books, 2008).

Rebecca McLaughlin, *Confronting Christianity: 12 Hard Questions for the World's Largest Religion* (Wheaton, IL: Crossway, 2019).

ABOUT THE AUTHOR

Tim Alsup has served as the Preaching Minister for the Great Oaks Church of Christ in Memphis, TN, since 2005.

Tim received a Doctor of Ministry (D. Min.) from Harding School of Theology in 2023, writing his dissertation on "Equipping Christians with a Post-Christian Evangelism Paradigm," the study on which this book is based. Prior to that, he completed two other graduate degrees: a Master of Divinity (M. Div.) from Harding (2015) and a Master of Arts (M.A.) in New Testament from Freed-Hardeman University (2005). His two undergraduate degrees were also from Freed-Hardeman (2002): a Bachelor of Arts (B.A.) in Bible and a Bachelor of Science (B.S.) in Mathematics.

Tim has written two other books:
- *Baptism 101: What the Bible Says About Baptism* (Gospel Advocate, 2010)
- *The Church of Christ: Pursuing God's Goals for His Church in a Divided Religious World* (Cross-Shaped Publishing, 2018)

Tim was born in Memphis, but grew up in Murfreesboro, TN. Outside of ministry, his hobbies include reading, sports, and spending time with family. His wife, Arinne, is originally from Benton, KY. They met as counselors at West Kentucky Youth Camp (a Christian camp in Marion, KY), dated at Freed-Hardeman University, and were married in Benton in December 2002. They have two boys and a girl: Riley, Eian, and Reese.